THREE BODLEY HEAD MONOGRAPHS

Arthur Ransome
HUGH SHELLEY

Rudyard Kipling
ROSEMARY SUTCLIFF

Walter de la Mare
LEONARD CLARK

THE BODLEY HEAD
LONDON SYDNEY
TORONTO

Acknowledgments are due to the Literary Trustees of Walter de la Mare for the quotations from the poetry and prose of Walter de la Mare.

SBN 370 00884 7
Arthur Ransome © Hugh Shelley 1960
Rudyard Kipling © Rosemary Sutcliff 1960
Walter de la Mare © Leonard Clark 1960
Printed and bound in Great Britain for
The Bodley Head Ltd
9 Bow Street, London WC2
by C. Tinling & Co. Ltd, Prescot
Set in Monotype Ehrhardt
First published, in three individual volumes, 1960
This edition, revised and re-set, 1968

Arthur Ransome

HUGH SHELLEY

CONTENTS

CONTENTS

1. Holidays and the Writer

There is a convention about monographs that they should be not merely objective but quite impersonal. Yet there can surely be no valid reason why 'a treatise embodying results of investigation of a single subject' should not be extremely personal; necessarily so in my own case, I submit, when the monograph concerns the books of Arthur Ransome.

Swallows and Amazons was first published in 1930. I was ten in the summer of that year—half way between the eldest and youngest active Swallow. It also happens that my father was a sailor, at that time a Commander in destroyers stationed in Malta; so was the Swallows' father—also a Commander, also out in Malta—the redoubtable Commander Walker, who sent his family a certain cable that altered the whole nature of their school holidays. School holidays, summer holidays; my life, like that of John, Susan, Titty and Roger Walker, centred round them.

Yet until Arthur Ransome, at the age of forty-six, wrote that now famous book that changed the course of so much children's literature, no one had treated school holidays as more than the setting of a novel. As Roger Lancelyn Green says,*

'there had been many stories of young people's holiday adventures before the coming of *Swallows and Amazons*, but usually these were humorous or mischievous or rather staid and serious.'

There had been on the serious side Mrs Molesworth's *The House that Grew* and, later, E. Nesbit's books. The

* *Tellers of Tales*, rev. ed. 1965.

latter were perhaps the true forerunners of Arthur Ransome's—certainly they were the first about children's life in the holidays to be written with some zest and humour—and it is interesting to learn that Arthur Ransome singled their author out as the only writer of children's books he could remember reading as a boy ... other than Robert Louis Stevenson. Oddly enough, the very first children's novel to be written with the object of entertaining rather than instructing the reader was Catherine Sinclair's *Holiday House*, published as far back as 1839, but it would be an unusual child who today could be passionately interested in her 'normal' children, beside whom Mrs Molesworth's appear young limbs of Satan.

Perhaps school holidays were not so important then. Certainly they were not for the girls who stayed at home all the year round with a governess. So despite the fact that one of the Sitwells once claimed to have been educated 'in the holidays from Eton', it is the last fifty years that have seen the real growth of the school holidays as the focal point of English children's interest.

The reason why Arthur Ransome became the Holidays' champion and chronicler is a very simple one; he spent the greater part of his life either looking forward to, enjoying or looking nostalgically back at them.

He was born in Leeds on January 18, 1884. His grandfather, a native of the Lake Country, was a not very successful scientist-inventor, but a first-rate field naturalist. His father, a professor of History in Yorkshire College (now Leeds University), was a real countryman—a keen fisherman and a very good shot. From the time Arthur Ransome was a baby the family spent all their holidays on a farm at the southern end of Coniston, for his mother shared her husband's affection for the Lake Country. The children (two boys and two girls) of whom Arthur Ransome was the eldest, used to swim, row and fish on the lake; to picnic on Peel Island, and to play and walk on the fells, making friends with farmers and shepherds, woodcutters and charcoal-burners. It was the enchanted, the magic place of which they dreamt while away from it.

Arthur Ransome was sent to a prep school in Windermere. He was not happy at school but he remembered with joy the Great Frost when the boys, instead of working in class-rooms, were allowed to play all day in the snow and to learn to skate while the lake remained frozen from end to end.

As a small boy, Arthur Ransome decided that he wanted to write books, but the idea was not encouraged by his parents. His father died just before he entered his public school, Rugby, and he was made to feel that, as the eldest of the family, he should become self-supporting as soon as possible. When he left school at seventeen, he still wanted to write but his mother argued that he must find a 'safe' job. He got work as a minor clerk, or glorified office boy, with a London firm of book publishers, Grant Richards. The hours were long and the pay meagre, but he was happy to be working among books and he spent every minute of his spare time reading and writing. For the first holiday he could afford he went on his own to Coniston, where he met W. G. Collingwood.* This was a fortunate meeting for the young man, and he subsequently spent many holidays with the Collingwood family, whose tastes and interests were similar to his own and who gave him stimulus and en-couragement. Collingwood, geologist and archaeologist, and an authority on the Scandinavian sagas, was a devoted friend to Ruskin (who had a house nearby; he is buried at

* Author of *Thorstein of the Mere*.

Coniston). Collingwood encouraged Ransome to persevere in his desire to write: with the two Collingwood girls (two and three years younger respectively) Ransome spent long days out of doors, walking, sketching and sailing, at times joined by their schoolboy brother Robin, with whom he later became friends. So it was that Arthur Ransome in young manhood relived the activities of his childhood holidays, and in so doing established a firm basis for the imaginative stories he wrote in middle age which brought him world-wide recognition. He was only twenty when his first book (a collection of articles) was published, but he always regretted this and wished he had been prevented from publishing anything until he was older.

He went to Russia in 1913 in order to study Russian folklore. Caught there at the outbreak of the First World War, he became successively War Correspondent for the *Daily News* and Special Correspondent for the *Manchester Guardian*. Except for short trips to England he lived in Russia until 1924, the last two years or so being spent in Estonia and Latvia (where *Racundra* was built). In 1925, he returned to England with his Russian wife and settled in a small cottage near Windermere; the lake was near enough for them to keep a boat and to spend at least one full day a week sailing and fishing, throughout the ten years they lived there. After this, Ransome made only a few excursions abroad. He wrote a weekly article on fishing for the *Manchester Guardian*, but he always looked on journalism as an interruption of his chosen career of writing books, and in 1929 (after the publication of *Racundra's First Cruise*) he gave it up altogether. The first five of the *Swallows and Amazons* series were written at the cottage near Lake Windermere.

In 1935 the Ransomes went to East Anglia—the part of

England he liked best after the Lake Country—and lived for five years close to the river Orwell. Here Arthur Ransome did a good deal of sailing. His own cruise to Holland was the basis of *We Didn't Mean to Go to Sea*; and Hamford Water (where he loved to spend a few quiet days at anchor) is the background of *Secret Water*. In 1940 the Ransomes returned to Coniston where they lived in a small house on the eastern shore of the lake until the end of the war. From 1946 they spent half of every year in a riverside flat in London and the other half on board a yacht on the South Coast, and later in an old farmhouse in the lakes, from which they could see Old Man Coniston. After a fall at the end of 1958, and the resulting severe illness, Arthur Ransome never completely regained his health. He died on June 3, 1967.

Throughout his life he had enjoyed holidays spent on the water. The last adult book he wrote before beginning the saga of the Swallows and the Amazons was *'Racundra's' First Cruise*, the story of his sailing the Baltic in a boat he had built on its shores, in the years immediately following the First World War. That curiously fascinating book does not really come within the scope of this monograph, which concerns his books specifically published (I will not say written) for children, but it should certainly appeal to many boys in their early teens, and it is of interest to the adult reader of the 'children's' books for the light it throws on its author's views on life in, out of and all around and about boats. It begins,

'Houses are but badly built boats so firmly aground that you cannot think of moving them. They are definitely inferior things, belonging to the vegetable not the animal world, rooted and stationary, incapable of gay transition.'

And Arthur Ransome's literary transitions, the transitions of all the boats in his books, *Swallow* and *Amazon*, *Death-*

and-Glory and *Titmouse*, *Wild Cat* and *Shining Moon*,
Sea Bear and *Goblin*, are fundamentally gay.

'The desire to build a house is the tired wish of a man
content thenceforward with a single anchorage. The desire
to build a boat is the desire of youth, unwilling yet to
accept the idea of a final resting place.'

I met Arthur Ransome at only two periods of his life, and
both of them late. The first was in 1952 when he blew in to
the bookshop I had with a friend in Littlehampton. I say
'blew in' advisedly, for he was in full sail under a volumin-
ous oilskin, a nautical Chesterton. And he had come down
to Littlehampton because, within hailing distance of seventy,
he was building yet another boat. The next time I saw him
was in 1959, when an accident sadly kept him for the
summer (mostly in bed) in London, and he could not
return to the Lakes. Yet even in London he was by water.
His windows overlooked the Thames at Putney, where small
boys in canoes, small boys optimistically fishing and large
men rowing, little knew under what accurate observation
they messed about in boats.

From boats, he turned, as a *pis aller*, to camping. Boats
come into *all* the books, but there are regrettable if un-
avoidable occasions when they are laid up and their sailors
cannot be waterborne all summer. The only alternative to the
ignominy of ordinary life, 'civilised' life, or as the children
so happily call it, 'native' life, is to have canvas rather than
plaster and slate between themselves and the sky. And, as in
The Picts and the Martyrs, even a deserted stone hut proved
better than a four-square modern residence with all the usual
comforts, sit-down meals and the wrong sort of aunt.

We have established one thing at least: not just holidays
but the right sort of holidays are the setting and in great
part the substance of Arthur Ransome's books.

II. Characters and Character

Arthur Ransome's twelve books 'for children' are really twelve volumes of one major work, as are the novels that compose the Forsyte Saga or the Doctor Dolittle books. The holidays they chronicle are consecutive and the Swallows and Amazons of the first volumes appear, sometimes separately, sometimes together, in most of the others. The Swallows, as I have mentioned, are the Walker Family, who are allowed to use the little sailing dinghy, *Swallow*. They appear in nine of the volumes, while their rivals and friends, Nancy and Peggy Blackett, who own the *Amazon*, also appear in nine. The two books in which neither family appears, *Coot Club* and *The Big Six*, set on the Norfolk Broads, both feature 'the 2 D's', Dick and Dorothea Callum, who are later friends of the Swallows and the Amazons, and share their adventures in four of the other books.

The children grow naturally older volume by volume, and the (fictional) lapse of time between *Swallows and Amazons* and *Great Northern?* is between five and six years. For this reason, because the author is constantly referring to occasions and characters in previous books, and because both style and subject matter are simplest in the early books, would-be readers are strongly recommended to begin at the beginning, with *Swallows and Amazons*. Which is what I propose to do in discussing first the heroes and heroines of the saga.

The Walker children arrive with their mother to spend their summer holidays at a farm on the shores of 'the Lake' in the Lake District. It is basically Lake Windermere, but for the purposes of the story it has borrowed one or two features from Lake Coniston—Peel Island, in particular. Peel Island, re-christened Wild Cat Island, is the focal point of *Swallows and Amazons*. Of course it had to be an island, accessible only by boat, and that, for the Walkers, could only mean a sailing boat.

The book opens in classic fashion,

'Roger, aged seven, and no longer the youngest of the family, ran in wide zig-zags, to and fro, across the steep field that sloped up from the lake to Holly Howe, the farm where they were staying for part of the summer holidays. . . . The wind was against him, and he was tacking up against it to the farm, where at the gate his patient mother was awaiting him. He could not run straight against the wind because he was a sailing vessel, a tea-clipper, the *Cutty Sark*.'

Mrs Walker had a telegram form in her hand. It was in answer to her query whether the children, John, Susan, Titty and Roger, should be allowed to sail in *Swallow*, a thirteen-foot dinghy, to Wild Cat Island, and camp there *all by themselves*. The now historic cable she received from her husband, Commander Walker, in Malta, read,

'BETTER DROWNED THAN DUFFERS
IF NOT DUFFERS WONT DROWN'

So the Walkers sat down and composed their ship's articles:

Master : John Walker
Mate : Susan Walker
Able-seaman : Titty Walker
Ship's Boy : Roger'

That was in the summer of 1930. And for the next seventeen years (in the telling—as opposed to the five or six years of the saga's own chronology) they are still the

Master, or Captain; the Mate; the Able-seaman and the Ship's Boy. And hundreds of thousands of children will have played their parts.

Who *are* the book's children? Did they really exist? Are their prototypes now middle-aged mariners? Apparently the reading public still believes that novelists' characters are invariably drawn from life, and legends about the 'originals' of the Walkers and the Blacketts are in constant circulation. There does indeed exist a family of four sisters and a brother, to whom *Swallows and Amazons* is dedicated —'in exchange for a pair of slippers'. It is not, however, true, as many people have imagined, that Arthur Ransome wrote his books *about* this family. In actual fact it was his memories of his own childhood and early youth spent in and out of boats on his beloved Coniston which were the true inspiration of the stories and their characters.

It is Arthur Ransome's triumph that both the background and characters of his books become so real to their readers, that people insist that there must have been models for both. Indeed, Arthur Ransome wrote,

'I know the geography of the country in the books so well that when I walk about in actual fact, it sometimes seems to me that some giant or earthquake has been doing a little scene shifting overnight.'*

His characters are even more lifelike, lively and memorable. The Amazons, who are not mere visiting holiday-makers like the Swallows but actually have the luck to live on the shores of the Lake, are Nancy and Peggy Blackett. Peggy is a normally healthy and sporting girl, but she shrinks to an insignificant, docile pawn, with neither mind nor will of her own beside her outrageous elder sister.

* *Junior Bookshelf*, Vol. 1, 4 (A letter to the Editor).

Nancy is the tomboy of tomboys, the utterly uninhibited leader, whom all the others follow without question, the complete extrovert, who leaves her contemporaries and her elders breathless and speechless.

' "Jib-booms and bobstays!" shouted Nancy Blackett, violently wrestling with a screw in one of her skates. "Nobody could beat those signals." '

The above quotation from *Winter Holiday* exemplifies her overpowering enthusiasm and energy. She could belong to no other sex, nation or background.

' "*Mille millions de sabords!*" the French translator makes her exclaim, '*tout en battant avec un des écrous de ses patins*, "*Ces signaux sont tout simplement formidables.*" '

Somehow, it just doesn't ring true! And as Nancy cannot be translated into a foreign language, so as a character one feels she could not be transmuted into a satisfactory, normal adult. One of Arthur Ransome's correspondents amused herself trying to imagine the future of the Swallows and the Amazons when they grew up. All, she felt, would be happy, with the exception of Nancy. She probably excelled herself in the war as a WREN, but afterwards . . . ? No, it is best to think of her for ever on the brink of her teens, at the helm of her ship, ever enthusiastic, resourceful and defiant.

The second strongest character of the books, and he, too, makes his appearance in the first, is, oddly enough, an adult. This is the Blacketts' idiosyncratic Uncle Jim, re-christened by the Walkers, 'Captain Flint', for they believe him to be a retired pirate. His is to no small extent a self-portrait. He is large and rather bald and disguised only by the absence of his creator's very fine (and once piratical) moustache. He is a rover, a sailor, a writer, an angler and a would-be solitary. Being irascible by nature, and certainly no besotted child lover, he is extremely put out when he is led to believe that the young are deliberately annoying him. This is one of the principal themes of *Swallows and Amazons*. Uncle Jim grossly misjudges the Swallows and is despicably unfair to them. When he discovers his mistake, he is immediately and most honourably remorseful, makes the fullest, most generous amends, and from that minute on becomes an honorary uncle to the Walkers and is the only adult allowed to share their and the Blacketts' adventures in subsequent books. Amiable, omniscient bachelor uncles on the side of the children rather than of their parents, have long been commonplaces of children's fiction. But Uncle Jim is the doyen of them all, besides being by far the most convincing.

While Nancy Blackett is the moving spirit behind the Swallows' and Amazons' adventures, and Uncle Jim their benevolent and beneficent supporter, who can give the sanction and aid without which parental opposition would scotch their plans, it is the Walkers who are the real heroes of the saga, with whom the reader must identify him- (or her-) self. It is more than an incidental pleasure to discover that Arthur Ransome, unlike the majority of his contemporaries writing for children, does not pander to the ten-year-old's article of faith that all females, bar 'sporting' mothers and aunts, are inexcusable interlopers in a world created by Dr Arnold.

The eldest Walker, Captain John, is their serious-minded leader. He is a thoroughly nice boy, who is determined to be a credit to his father and is the most nautically minded and knowledgeable of the five. It is a slight surprise to find him still at school in his teens and not at Dartmouth. The eldest girl, Mate Susan, is the domestically-minded one who sees to it that the others have enough to eat and wear, and, if they get their feet wet, change their socks or put on their plimsolls. She is almost a 'native', as the children call the adults. The next girl, Titty, is a complete contrast. Although she is anxious to be as good a sailor as John, and could not bear anyone to think her feeble, she is by nature an unpractical dreamer (to those who despise her) or, as her family and friends happily admit, the only one with a properly developed imagination and sensibility. She sees dangers that the others ignore, and yet she conquers a natural timidity far stronger than theirs to help overcome them. Roger, the youngest active Swallow, until (in *Secret Water*) the baby, Bridget, becomes old enough to join the party, is—again by contrast—an amiably simple character. He thinks of only two things: engines (he refuses to kotow to his brother's and sisters' god of canvas) and food. The latter, whether it be the next meal, snack or bar of chocolate.

There are two other major characters, but they do not appear until the fourth volume, *Winter Holiday*, where they join forces with the Walkers and the Blacketts. These are Dick and Dorothea Callum. She is a literary romantic and a writer, at first slightly despised, or at any rate disregarded by the Swallows and Amazons, but finally accepted for her courageous support of what to most children would be a freak of a brother. Dick is studiously scientific, 'a swot', in the eyes of his generation. It is to Arthur Ransome's very great credit that, as another critic has already remarked, Dick never degenerates into a clown. He could so easily have become the buffoon of the party. Instead, the peaceable Roger is only too ready to be laughed at for his concentration on what at that era was a 'tuppenny bar', while Dick, in the very last book, the last volume of the saga, *Great Northern?*, becomes the acknowledged hero, and—even Nancy tacitly admits it—the real leader of them all.

Those readers for whom this short monograph is their

first introduction to the name of Ransome may well be puzzled at such emphasis on the characters in his books, when their content has been discussed only in very general terms. However, so many reviewers and critics have praised the books primarily for their plots that people forget that the distinction of Arthur Ransome as a writer for children lies not in telling 'rattling good yarns' and becoming a twentieth-century Ballantyne, but in his ability to write about children who were not only credible, attractive individuals who grew up as they grew older, but also personalities with whom at least a million children have been able to identify themselves. In subsequent chapters we can consider the plots and substance of all the twelve volumes, but always in connection with the principals and the supporting cast.

III. The First Two of the Twelve

Swallows and Amazons is not the most professional of the twelve books, but in many ways it is the most endearing, the friendliest. Re-reading it as an adult, one senses the enjoyment and the enthusiastic application with which it was written. For great children's books, unlike the majority of great books for adults, have had joy in—at any rate in the early stages—their making. Lewis Carroll would have enjoyed at least the first telling of Alice's adventures; Kenneth Grahame would have delighted in his letters to 'Mouse'. And as these tales would have been a relaxation to the former after his mathematical text books and to the latter after the daily business of the Bank of England, so the composition of *Swallows and Amazons* must have been a delight after a score of books of essays, literary criticism, and political studies of the U.S.S.R. and China, for Arthur Ransome, as I shall mention in more detail later, was a professional writer for *a quarter of a century* before he wrote his first book that made his name as a writer for children.

The Swallows, as I have explained, land on Wild Cat Island. The grown-ups, the natives, are satisfactorily cut off and unable to interfere, and so the children are free to do exactly as they wish. But whereas a lesser writer would have plunged straightway into action and adventure, this leisurely tyro among children's writers is quite content to let his Swallows explore the island, set up camp, eat and drink, swim and fish for four whole chapters.

When adventure comes, it is in the very tame form of the arrival of the Amazons. A brief skirmish, a parley, and

Swallows and Amazons take to each other and make a treaty. It is lucky they do, for the Blacketts' Uncle Jim, Captain Flint, is under the misapprehension that the Walkers have been raiding the ancient pleasure steamer turned houseboat in which he periodically lives and tries to work. The true villains had been his own nieces who, angered by their uncle's recent withdrawal into native life, had thrown fireworks on to the old hulk's roof. Soon, however, real thieves board and break into the houseboat. They steal the only object that looks as though it might contain valuables, an old cabin trunk. The contents, however, are neither money nor jewels, but the manuscript of Uncle Jim's book of reminiscences. It is rediscovered thanks entirely to Titty— Titty, who, when Swallows and Amazons plan a mock battle, overcomes her fear of being left alone on the island, manages to capture the *Amazon*, and spending the night in her off a deserted shore hears the sounds of men burying something. The rediscovery of the trunk and manuscript crowns a reconciliation with Uncle Jim, who makes up for ill-natured, unjustified mistrust of the Swallows by organis- ing a grand finale of a battle: Swallows and Amazons *versus* the Houseboat, boarding it in approved piratical fashion and making its captain actually walk the plank. The summer holidays are over and, one perfect late summer evening, the *Swallow* sails back to civilisation, her crew all singing,

'Oh, soon wc'll hear the Old Man say,
"Leave her, Johnny, leave her." '

until land and 'natives' heave in sight once more.

'"Who *was* Johnny?" said Roger. "Hullo, there's mother and Vicky coming down the field." '

* * *

The successor and sequel to *Swallows and Amazons* is

23

Swallowdale, and what a worthy, satisfying sequel it is. It has the same endearing quality, the same characters and the same setting; it is better written and more exciting.

It is longer too, and by today's standards exceptionally so. Indeed, returning to Ransome after reading more recent children's books, one is struck by the length of his stories. Admittedly, *Swallowdale* is the longest, nearly 150,000 words, but they are all long. Whereas nowadays a children's novel of 60,000 words is quite usual, the shortest Ransome, *The Picts and the Martyrs*, is 64,000 and the average is nearly 90,000. It is astonishing to think that they came out at 7s 6d, (with roughly 26 full-page illustrations and many tailpieces) and that today each costs only 15s or 16s.

The period of *Swallowdale* is the Walkers' second summer in the Lake District, the very next year after their adventures in *Swallow* and *Amazon* and on Wild Cat Island. Roger is now eight; the baby, Vicky, is a toddler and henceforth known by her proper name of Bridget; and they are all much more sure of themselves. Too sure, alas, for right at the beginning of the holidays the Swallows are sailing in a strong wind, when John fails to reef, and runs *Swallow* on Pike rock, where she is holed and sunk. They manage to salvage her without adult aid, but she is a case for the boat-yards, there can be no sailing to the Island this summer; they must find alternative excitement.

Philosophically, they explore the hills, find a Secret Valley and climb 'Kanchenjunga' (the Old Man of Coniston, in geographical fact). And there are many other adventures before *Swallow* is repaired and, in the last two chapters, they are once more racing *Amazon*. The Amazons, incidentally, play a smaller part than hitherto, for they (and poor Uncle Jim as well) have 'native trouble', in the shape of an impossibly pernickety Great Aunt.

Sad though this may be for Nancy's admirers, we do get to know the Walkers far better. By the end of the book they are as familiar as our closest friends, not only because Arthur Ransome identifies himself and makes us identify ourselves with them, but because he takes time over them. As in *Swallows and Amazons*, there is no rush to get on with the story. Pages are spent in describing the daily, even the hourly, life of the children. Susan, at her most 'native', reminds them of their holiday tasks and Titty doggedly takes her French Grammar out one morning.

'She had a pretty firm hold on *J'ai, tu as, il a* but was still muddled with *avais* and *aviez* and *avaient* and lost hope altogether when it came to *eus, eut, eûmes* and *eurent*.'

And when Susan cooks, there is a detailed description of the best way to make buttered eggs, or to cook fish in camp. Many girls and boys, one hopes, remember her mother's advice to her in *Swallows and Amazons* that if you want to like cooking, you must make the others wash up.

The other agreeably effective way in which Arthur Ransome brings one to know his characters is by frequent back reference. They are continually remembering, as children do, what happened the last time they were in such-and-such a place or predicament. The children are worth getting to know, because they always behave as children and not as cardboard heroes. The place or predicament is never taken in the children's stride as it usually is in the second-rate adventure story. They are ever new and strange; unfamiliar and little frequented country can be very un-nerving to children, and Arthur Ransome knows this well. The Walkers and the Blacketts get tired and hungry and feel lonely as children do. And from time to time, their tiredness, hunger and loneliness are such that only adults can assuage them. How different from those heroes and heroines of Cornish cove mysteries, who can retrieve the school cups, unmask the villain and uncover an international spy ring in twenty-four sleepless, foodless, waterless hours. Arthur Ransome is sufficiently familiar with physical discomfort and the disadvantages of solitude to appreciate two major facts of childhood: achievement in the face of ungauged difficulties and hardships is the most exciting thing; loneliness with neither physical nor moral support is the most daunting. In *Swallows and Amazons*, one of the best passages describes how Titty makes up her mind to stay alone on the Island and play her lone part in the night battle between the Amazon pirates and the crew of the *Swallow* rather than take her mother's offer of a row home to civilisation. In *Swallowdale* it is Titty again who is left alone, this time with a frightened Roger, when the two of them lose their way on the moors in the fog. Roger sprains his ankle—and they have eaten the last of the chocolate. The blackest moment is pictured thus,

' "We must have gone an awful long way to the right," said the Boy.

"It can't be much farther now," said the Able-seaman.

And then, suddenly, their cheerfulness came to an end.

"Look," said Roger, who was a yard or two ahead, "there's a tree! On the other side. I'm going to cross."

"There aren't any trees," said Titty.

"I can see it. It's a big one," said Roger, and jumped.

He landed with a short squeak of pain on the other side. His left foot slipped between two stones and twisted over. He fell forward, tried to pick himself up, squeaked again and flopped on the ground.

"Have you hurt yourself?" asked Titty, jumping across the stream.

"Rather," said the Boy.

"Badly?"

"Very badly. I can't get up. But I was right about the tree. Look at it."

If Roger had something in his mind, nothing would stop him from talking of it. He had been thinking of the tree before he jumped. He was thinking of it still, as he lay beside the stream. Titty looked up.

Close above them a tall pine towered like a grey ghost in the white mist. Titty was almost as much troubled by the tree as by Roger.

"There are no trees on top of the moor," she said. "There aren't any till down on the other side of Swallowdale in the wood above Swainson's Farm."

"Well, there it is," said Roger. "Ouch!"

"Where does it hurt?"

"It's my best foot. Broken, I think."

"Oh, Roger."

"And there is no more chocolate." '

Roger is occasionally fanciful and often slightly—naturally—silly, while Titty is blessed and cursed with the most vivid of imaginations. Both are determined to overcome their several fears. Whenever they are successful, their heroism is in accordance with their age; their achievements are triumphs of their age. They are genuine heroes.

IV. Forerunners, Fairy Tales and Fantasy

Before continuing to follow in the Swallows' and Amazons' wake, it is worth stopping to consider how Arthur Ransome, by nature a romantic and by training and upbringing a practical man, by nature imaginative and by profession and often by inclination a factual man, should have come to make his name by writing books that have been welcomed by the young of so many different nations.

How did he become a writer? He has answered this question himself.

'Until I was about eight years old,' he tells us, 'I was a cheerful small boy of action rather than of letters. Then one day we were playing at ships under and on a big dining-room table which had underneath it, in the middle, a heavy iron screw pointing downwards. It was my watch below. My brother or sister was on the bridge, on top of the table, and suddenly raised a shout for "All hands on deck!" I started up, and that big screw under the middle of the table made a most horrible dent in my skull, altered its shape and so, in one moment, changed my character for life. I crawled out, much shaken; and that very afternoon wrote my first book, about a desert island, in a little notebook with a blue cover. I have been writing ever since.'

After leaving school, he went to London and worked in a publishing house. From that insecure bridgehead he made forays into the literary world. By the age of twenty-one, he had published two small volumes of short pieces that had appeared in various periodicals, and in 1907, when he was

28

twenty-three, he wrote *Bohemia in London*, a charming, if occasionally mannered, and nostalgic, almost elderly, book of reminiscences about his own and others' literary life in the capital just three years previously! After editing *The World's Story-tellers* for T. C. & E. C. Jack, he put together for them his first full-length book, *A History of Story-telling*. This paved the way for a study of Edgar Allan Poe and another of Oscar Wilde. Arthur Ransome spent much time experimenting with the techniques of story-telling, and the later books of reportage on China and Russia that he wrote in the 1920s as well as his one book on sailing, '*Racundra*'*s' First Cruise*, and his first collection of fishing articles, *Rod and Line*, gave him experience in writing economically and accurately as well as fluently. It is perhaps worth noting that Arthur Ransome's second collection of fishing essays, *Mainly about Fishing*, which appeared as late as February 1959, is every whit as vigorous and delightful as its predecessor published thirty years earlier. It is a pleasure to the uninstructed, and evidently to the expert; in the periodical *Angling*, the reviewer remarked that it 'joins the group of books that are read again and again, in whole or part, as long as eyesight lasts.'

As can be seen from the bibliography at the end of this monograph, Arthur Ransome wrote many more books for adults than I have mentioned, and I shall not attempt to discuss the very considerable quantity of his work that appeared only in periodicals. He also wrote some fairy stories that were, he says, 'as bad as they could be'. There are, however, two children's books outside the Swallow and Amazon saga that are worth consideration. In 1919 appeared his rhymed version of *Aladdin*. After a merrily defiant dedication to Lascelles Abercrombie, he launches out into,

'The wind blows through the bamboo wood,
The coloured lanterns swing and gleam,
And sleeping Chinese children dream
Of small Aladdin and his Djinns.'

It is a handsome crown quarto, with Dulac-like illustrations by Mackenzie; the story is told with despatch and humour in fine, spanking verse, with an occasional surprising subtlety of rhythm; and many parents must have read it to their children with zest. It has been out of print for many years.

* * *

The other book is a very different matter; it has been in print for over half a century. *Old Peter's Russian Tales* was first published in 1916 and since then has been continuously read, and enjoyed, by children and storytellers alike.

In his Note to the first edition, Arthur Ransome said,

'I think there must be more fairy stories told in Russia than anywhere else in the world. In this book are a few of those I like best. I have taken my own way with them more or less, writing them mostly from memory.'

He had started by trying to translate them direct from the Russian, but discovered that straightforward translations were unsatisfactory; children found them difficult and dull. So he retold them in words which he put into the mouth of an old Russian peasant, Peter, who lives with his two grandchildren in the heart of the forest. The two children, Vanya and Maroosia, ask him to tell them the tales to while away the long winter evenings. The practical details and working of machines and contraptions, gadgets and gilhickies, that are such a feature of the later books are foreshadowed in the natural way Arthur Ransome introduces incidental details of country life in old Russia: stuffing the window with moss to keep out the cold, the size and shape of the stove, the detailed description of the hay-cushioned wooden cart in which the children drive to the village, of a baby's cradle, and of a samovar and how it is used.

The stories themselves are delightfully told and suit Arthur Ransome's taste in humour and for colour and magic. *Baba Yaga*, *The Fire Bird*, *Frost*, *The Fool of the World* and *The Cat who became Head-forester* are some of the twenty-one folk tales in the book that the people of the Russian countryside have passed down to each other for generations.

* * *

The two books in the Swallow and Amazon saga that most closely resemble Arthur Ransome's earlier writings are *Peter Duck* and *Missee Lee*. These differ from the other ten books in that they are imaginary adventures supposedly invented by the Swallows and the Amazons to beguile winter evenings between their own summer holiday adventures. They are said to have been told on board a wherry, hired by Uncle Jim for them all to spend their Christmas holidays in on the Norfolk Broads. Their principal creator was naturally made out to be Titty.

Peter Duck, although published in 1932, after *Swallowdale*, was actually planned before it, as observant readers of the latter will have divined. In *Swallowdale* there are several references to Titty's imaginary friend,

'Peter Duck had grown up gradually to be one of the Able-seaman's most constant companions, shared now and then by the Boy, but not taken very seriously by the others, though nobody laughed at him. . . . Peter Duck, who said he had been afloat ever since he was a duckling, was the old

31

sailor who had voyaged with them to the Caribees in the story and, still in the story, had come back to Lowestoft with his pockets full of pirate gold.'

After seeing the photograph in '*Racundra's*' *First Cruise*, one feels that he must to some extent have been based on 'The Ancient Mariner', the classic (Baltic) old salt, who crew'd for Arthur Ransome on that voyage, while his wife presided over the galley.

Both *Peter Duck* and *Missee Lee* give Arthur Ransome full opportunity to indulge his taste for credibly outrageous fantasy. In *Peter Duck*, Captain Flint takes the Walkers, the Blacketts and the aforementioned 'ancient' to the Caribbean, racing the scoundrelly Black Jake and his crew aboard the *Viper* for the treasure buried in Crab Island. In *Missee Lee*, they sail out of their hundredth port and into trouble in the China Sea; they are captured by a superbly logical, implacable and highly cultured pirate captain: Missee Lee herself. (After mentioning the samovar in *Old Peter's Russian Tales*, it would be a pity not to draw attention to the tailpiece to Chapter IX. It is entitled, 'How to eat with chopsticks'.)

The originality of *Peter Duck* and *Missee Lee* compared with the bulk of fantasies for the young lies, paradoxically, in the convincing background of factual detail. Often the author shows more concern with the mechanics of 'going foreign' than he does in the stories of the Swallows and the Amazons with the technicalities of sailing. *Peter Duck*, for example, contains detailed drawings of the ship in which they sail to the Caribbean, and Arthur Ransome tells how he carefully worked out the course from Lowestoft to 'Crab Island' so that the adventurous could actually sail there and back with the aid of the text and the end-paper map. As for *Missee Lee*, the author had been to China, having been sent there by the *Manchester Guardian* at the time of the Chinese Revolution, and had subsequently written *Chinese Puzzle*.

Even more striking than the accuracy of the background is the consistency with which the children, in their own story, the one they made up, behave exactly as they would under the story's circumstances. With a sigh of relief one realises that it would be blowhard Nancy, by all the barbecued billygoats in the northern hemisphere, who was overwhelmingly seasick as the *Wild Cat* lurched south down the North Sea. It is an agreeable surprise that the desperately keen John should be less confident than he was on the Lake. At one point Captain Flint called him to take over the wheel and,

'John gulped, but said "Aye, aye, sir," as stoutly as he could. A moment later he was feeling the ship, meeting her as she yawed, looking anxiously back at her rather waggly wake, and trying to do with a real ship at sea what he had learnt to do very well with the little *Swallow* on the Lake in the North.'

v. Children with Adults

Personally, I am glad to get back to the Lake in the North, to Coniston-Windermere, as Arthur Ransome's ability to create fantastic reality is to me more exciting than his admittedly remarkable achievement in writing realistic fantasy.

The other books about the Lake are *Winter Holiday*, *Pigeon Post* and *The Picts and the Martyrs*. The first two are early; *Winter Holiday* follows immediately after *Swallowdale* in both factual and fictional time, and only *Coot Club* comes between *Winter Holiday* and *Pigeon Post*. *The Picts and the Martyrs* is the penultimate volume of the twelve and the shortest. It is also, I think, the least successful. Ransomanes are so far united in refusing to criticise any of 'the twelve', but I must risk their giving me the black spot as Nancy memorably gave it to Captain Flint, by suggesting that we are brought back to the Lake—after sorties into strange parts of the British Isles—a little under false pretences. The plot mainly concerns the efforts of the Amazons and the 2 D's to outwit the abominable Great Aunt, whom we had not met since *Swallowdale*. But perhaps I am prejudiced by the absence of the Swallows.

The 2 D's, Dick and Dorothea Callum, first enter the saga in *Winter Holiday*. They happen to be staying at Dixon's farm, so it is inevitable that they should meet the Walkers and the Blacketts, spending their winter holidays respectively at Holly Howe and Beckfoot. As I have mentioned, they are a scientifically minded, very serious boy and his literary younger sister. There is something rather pathetic

ARTHUR RANSOME

about their dogged loyalty respectively to fact and fiction
and to each other. Both are frightened of being thought
duffers and their great ambition is to be approved by (or
at least to pass muster with) such obviously capable
children as the Blacketts and the Walkers.

The Lake is almost as attractive in winter as in summer,
particularly as it freezes solid,* Nancy goes down with
mumps, and as all the rest are in quarantine, the holidays
are prolonged. The story is about an expedition they plan
to make by sledge to 'the North Pole', the farthest northern
shore of the Lake. Captain Flint's houseboat is iced up and
becomes the *Fram* (Nansen's ship) acting as the expedition's
headquarters until Nancy is well again and they can all set
off.

Captain Flint returns unexpectedly from abroad and at
once enters into the spirit of the expedition. By now the
position of the grown-ups in the stories has become clearly
defined. Strangers who merely happen to cross the children's
horizon are imagined to be something else that will not spoil
the fantasy of their adventures. The skaters on the frozen
Lake that has become the Arctic Ocean encasing the *Fram*,
are counted as Eskimoes or seals, just as in *Swallowdale*,
when Titty and Roger went off exploring on their own, the
hooting cars on the main road became trumpeting savages.
Adults within the children's family circle become 'natives'
for the purposes of fantasy, but they are acknowledged to
have 'real' lives as well. All of them (with the exception of
that Great Aunt) are remarkably good-natured and willing
to give the children what assistance they can to make the
games, adventures and expeditions a success. Uncle Jim is
their mainstay, but the others help staunchly. At times, there

* As it did in fact when Arthur Ransome, a small boy, was at school at
Windermere in the early 'nineties.

is an almost feudal atmosphere, for not only parents and other relations join in, but the lower orders* play their part. One is forcibly reminded that the first books were written in the early 'thirties, when class distinctions still survived in England. However, one feels that the farmers' wives who lodge the children and the various locals they meet are friendly only because they are amused by and like the children. Other characters, such as the two Billies, the charcoal burners who appear in both *Swallows and Amazons* and *Swallowdale*, Mary Swainson in *Swallowdale*, and others, are all pleasant open folk. Their deference is the natural, often protective, politeness of country people. What is more, they are never mere ciphers; they have definite characters, unlike the background yokels of so many children's books. And their dialect, unlike the Mummerset of fictional coastguards, has the ring of authenticity. One of the nicest of Arthur Ransome's Westmorlanders (or northern Lancastrians) is Mr Dixon, the farmer who speaks to no one until the Callums appear on the scene, when he and Dick strike up a convincingly odd friendship that astonishes even Mrs Dixon.

On the whole, though, the children's relations with the adult world are a minor matter. It is their relationship with each other and their development that is most interesting. Some, like Susan and Roger, are simple characters, so simple that adult readers may weary of the constant repetition of their not very subtle characteristics. Susan's 'native' mind, her preoccupation with the domestic economy of each expedition and adventure, its victualling, health and hygiene, is constantly reiterated, while Roger's ever-empty stomach and thoughts of chocolate recur in book after book. But these repetitions are not solely for the sake of opposing

* *'In the Lake country there are no "lower orders".'*—Arthur Ransome.

Susan's practical to Nancy's adventurous, Dorothea's romantic and Titty's imaginative approach, or, for that matter, of bringing in Roger's unworthy pangs as light relief. Children love repetition, both comic repetition (which, of course, is a basic ingredient of the most primitive comedy) and serious repetition that gives the sense of continuity and security their conservative natures require. If one can remember one's own favourite books as a child, it is not hard to understand what the little girl meant when she asked Arthur Ransome to write another book exactly like the last 'with the same people and the same places and all the same things happening'.

VI. *Pigeon Post*

Pigeon Post, sixth of the series, and one of the most complete, is an outstanding example of Arthur Ransome's ability not only to analyse character and show its development but to do so dramatically. And in terms any boy or girl of average sensitivity can appreciate.

Pigeon Post was the first book to win the now famous Carnegie Medal. The Medal was instituted by the Library Association and awarded to Arthur Ransome in 1936, not so much, one is given to understand, for his achievement in *Pigeon Post* itself, but to honour the man who was unquestionably the foremost English children's writer at the time. *Swallows and Amazons*, *Swallowdale*, *Peter Duck*, *Winter Holiday* and *Coot Club* were the books it crowned. Because of this *Pigeon Post* and its successors are often underrated. Not, I am glad to say by all critics. In his *Twentieth Century Children's Books*, Frank Eyre describes it as 'one of his best stories . . . a perfect model of how to write a children's story, for in it he subjects his group of children to all the superficial ingredients of the conventional children's "thriller". There is a mysterious stranger, a search for treasure, midnight excursions and so on; but how skilfully it is all handled and how differently the children themselves react. And yet how much more truly exciting it is than the usual nonsense.'

The 'miners' camp', sought by the 'prospectors', is threatened from various quarters. First, the Blacketts' mother feels that they are all going too far afield for her to feel happy about them, and this is where the pigeons come

in. The children release them at intervals to reassure
her that they are all right. Then lack of water makes their
chosen camping ground unfeasible and they have to put up
their tents in an orchard in the lee of the most civilised of
farms. I was in error when I said that all grown-ups bar the
Great Aunt were sympathetic. Mrs Tyson is the queen of
uncomprehending adult females; instead of leaving them to
fend for themselves and cook in their own billycans over
their own fires, she prepares admirably sustaining suppers
and makes them feel ashamed of being five minutes late
for them.

There is only one way out; they *must* find water near their
chosen camping site. Hopes are raised when Dick finds
rushes that grow only where there is water. If only one of
them were a born dowser. . . . They all try with a hazel
twig, but it is no good. The irrepressible Roger is fooling
around 'discovering' planted jam jars of water, when they
realise Titty hasn't had a go. They give her the stick and
she sets off.

'"Half a minute," said Captain Nancy eagerly. "Didn't
it give a sort of jerk just now?"

Titty looked round miserably. "It can't have," she said.

"There it is again," said Nancy. "Look here. . . ."

Titty's eyes were swimming. She saw the ground of the
yard at her feet through a mist. Something queer was happening that she could neither help nor hinder. The stick
was more than a bit of wood in her hands. It was coming
alive. If only she could drop it, and be free from it. But
there was Captain Nancy's voice, talking, close to her and
yet far away. . . . The ends of the stick were lifting her
thumbs. She fought against them, trying as hard as she
could to hold them still. But the fork of the stick was
dipping, dipping. Nothing could stop it. Her hands turned

in spite of her. "Titty! Titty!" They were all talking to her at once. The next moment the stick had twisted clean out of her hands. It lay on the ground, just a forked hazel twig with the green showing through the bark where Nancy's knife had trimmed it. Titty, the dowser, startled more than she could bear, and shaking with sobs, had bolted up into the wood.'

All the others agreed that Titty must not be forced to dowse against her will, but after a dismal day that begins with Nancy going out alone to try with the twig—near a little puddle, round which the naturalist Dick had observed the tracks of some small animals—and ends with them all in black despair, Titty slips out after supper by herself.

'She had reached the top of the wood and the turning through the bushes to the old pitstead of the charcoal-burners when she heard a quick rustling of dried leaves and twigs. Something small was coming down to meet her. She pulled out her torch, but did not light it. The thing, whatever it was, was on the path close above her. She stood perfectly still. There it was. A rabbit? No. She knew now what it was that had left the muddy prints by the pool halfway down the hill. Steadily trotting down the path, now and then lifting its head to sniff, a hedgehog came hurrying in the dusk. He seemed to know that something strange was about, but he looked for things of his own height, and never saw Titty, towering above him. He passed close to her feet, carelessly, noisily hurrying down the path as if the wood belonged to him.

"He wants water, too," said Titty to herself. "And he's got to go down the hill for it, just like us. He'd be jolly glad if I did find any near the top."

She let the hedgehog get well below her, so as not to startle him, and then went on to the camp that might have been. There was more light in the open space that the charcoal-burners had cleared. Titty knew just where Nancy had thrown her forked twig in the morning. Nancy would be sure to cut the right twig. It would be better to try with that instead of looking for another.

She found the twig at once and picked it up by the point of the fork, putting off to the very last minute the holding of those two ends in her hands. But perhaps it would not work, anyway.

Titty swallowed once or twice. No one was here to see. No one would ever know if, after all, she could not bring herself to do it.

"Oh, come on," she said to herself. "You've got to. Better get it over."

She turned the twig round and took the two ends, one in each hand just as Nancy had shown her by Mrs Tyson's pump. She found herself breathing very fast.

"Duffer," she said firmly. "You can just drop it if you want."

She began walking to and fro across the level platform of the old fire spot. Nothing happened.

"Idiot," she said. "It won't be here, anyway."

She left the platform and went in among the trees, looking in the dim light for Dick's green rushes. She found a tuft of them. Still nothing happened.

"It's all right," she said to herself. "You can't do it. It was only an accident the other night. Nothing to be afraid of, anyway. And you've tried. So it wasn't your fault. . . ."

And then she nearly dropped the twig. There it was, that tickling. Not like the other night at Tyson's. But the same thing. The twig was trying to move.

For a long time she stood where she was, somehow not daring to stir. Then she took a step or two, and the stick was as dead as ever.

"This is silly," she said, and stepped back to the place where she had been and felt the stick press against the balls of her thumbs just as it had before.

41

"Well, it can't bite you," said Titty, and made herself walk to and fro, among the bushes and low trees at the edge of the wood just as she had on the open platform of Might Have Been.

The twig was moving again. Again it stopped. Again it twitched in her fingers.

"There *is* water here," said Titty to herself. "There must be. Unless it's all rot, like Dick thought."

She walked slowly on. The twig was pulling harder and harder. She wanted to throw it down, but somehow, by herself, she was not as frightened of it as she had been when, all unexpectedly, she had felt it for the first time. No one was watching her now, for one thing. She had won her battle the moment she had brought herself to hold the twig again. Now, already, she was almost eagerly feeling the pulling of the twig. When it weakened she moved back until she felt it strengthen. Then again she walked on. It was like looking for something hidden, while someone, who knew where it was, called out hot or cold as she moved nearer to or farther from the hiding place.

Suddenly, as she came nearer the Great Wall, the twisting of the twig became more violent. Here was a shallow dip in the ground between two rocks, and, yes, there was another tuft of those rushes in the bottom of it. She walked in between the rocks and it was just as it had been in the farmyard at Tyson's. The stick seemed to leap in her hands. The ends of it pressed against her thumbs, while the point of the fork dipped towards the ground, bending the branches, twisting her hands round with them, and at last almost springing out of her fingers.

"It's here," said Titty. "I've found it!" '

VII. Far Adventure

The first of the 'real' books to be set away from the Lake District—I except *Peter Duck*—is *Coot Club*, which is also the first to feature neither Swallows nor Amazons but only the 2 D's, whom we had just met for the first time in *Winter Holiday*. They go to spend their Easter holidays on the Norfolk Broads, where they meet the Coot Club. This is a local bird protection society consisting of Tom Dudgeon, an East Anglian doctor's son, and the 'Death and Glories', Jo, Pete and Bill, an intriguing trio, the sons of local boat builders. The story mostly concerns the Coot Club's war with a motor-cruiser load of vulgar landlubbers whom Tom Dudgeon cuts adrift from their mooring right on top of a nesting coot.

The 2 D's come to his aid when he is 'outlawed', and courageously put into practice what they have learned of boat-handling. This, of course, equips them for complete participation in future adventures with the expert Walkers and Blacketts.

We Didn't Mean to Go to Sea, the second of the 'non-Lake' books, and the successor to *Pigeon Post*, is the one I suspect Arthur Ransome himself considered his best. Certainly, it is the most exciting. The motto of the book (and an echo of the same phrase in *Pigeon Post*) is a dictum of Commander Walker, Royal Navy,

> 'Grab a chance and you won't be sorry for a might-have-been.'

Arthur Ransome considered that the greatest tribute ever

43

paid to him was Eric Hiscock's adopting this sentence for his motto and having it carved on the beam above the companionway of his *Wanderer III* before setting out in her on his round-the-world cruise.

The chance is a heaven-sent one for the Swallows to prove themselves in real difficulties and real danger in quite possible circumstances that could lead to disaster if anyone were to panic. Holidaying in East Anglia—Pin Mill and Shotley are the setting—they meet one Jim Brading who has just sailed his cutter, *Goblin*, up round the coast from Dover. He invites them to spend a night aboard, and while he is ashore fetching petrol for the auxiliary, she drags anchor and, in dense fog, with all the Walkers bar Bridget on board, drifts out to sea. She lands up, after a terrifying night, off Flushing—just as she would have done, for Arthur Ransome, with his passion for accuracy, checked the course by sailing his own yacht to Beach End buoy, letting her drift and then following the *Goblin*'s course.

The reality of the book lies, however, not in the plausibility of its plot, but in the naturalness of the children's behaviour, the effect such an experience has on each. The main interest is not in the situation but in the way the boys and girls react to it. There are no phoney heroics. They are sick as cats, Titty, early on, goes below with a splitting headache, Roger—quite naturally—is scared stiff, and Susan, the stolid domesticated Susan, is at one moment in a flood of tears. So one is not surprised that they make it, that they win through—and even rescue a shipwrecked kitten on the way.

At one point in the middle of the night, John realises that they are carrying too much sail. The wind has got up and they are pitching and tossing, but he determinedly inches along the deck to reef. Susan is left at the tiller.

'And then she saw him get to his feet and stand there, swaying with the leaping boat, with his hands on shrouds and halyards.

"John!" Her call was indignant. What on earth was he doing that for?

"John!" Her angry call turned unexpectedly into a call for help. She was going to be sick again. She choked. Something buzzed in her head. Spots dithered before her eyes. Yes. She was going to be sick now, at once. . . . He must come, quick, to take the tiller for her.

"John! . . . *Oh!*" Her call for help turned to a shriek of terror. John was gone. One moment he had been standing on the foredeck, swaying with the motion of the *Goblin*. The next moment he was gone. A clutching hand missing the shrouds . . . the life-line jerking taut. He was gone . . . '

When John regains the cockpit, he mentions the fact that he thought he heard her call out. Shamefacedly she says that she thought she was going to be sick.

' ". . . and John . . . it's very queer. I don't feel sea-sick any more."

"Good," said John. "Once it's over, you'll probably never be sea-sick again. How's Titty?" '

And that was that.

*   *   *

One might have thought that the subsequent books would be anticlimaxes, particularly as the next one, *Secret Water*, is about nothing more exciting than surveying. Commander Walker has returned from foreign parts—this time from the China station—and has for the first time entered the saga in person in *We Didn't Mean to Go to Sea*. His steamer, casting off from the quay in Flushing Harbour, passed the *Goblin* and he was put aboard just in time to share his children's very much smoother recrossing of the North Sea. He has returned for some well-earned leave in England, and one cannot help commenting that it seems to have been extraordinarily remiss of the Admiralty to have sent him straight from Malta to China without leave. However, it seems more than remiss of them, particularly in peace time, to cancel his leave at the beginning of *Secret Water* and insist that he take up his new shore appointment at Shotley, forthwith. How right that *Secret Water* should begin,

'The First Lord of the Admiralty was unpopular at Pin Mill.

"I hate him," said Roger, sitting on the foredeck of the *Goblin*, with his legs dangling over the side.

"Who?" said Titty.

"The first of those lords," said Roger.

"We all hate him," said Titty.'

As Commander Walker cannot spend his children's next holidays with them, he takes them off by boat to camp up an unfrequented East Anglian creek (Hamford Water was the original) on what is an island at high water and a mud-encompassed peninsula at low water. The object of the expedition is to chart the area, which they do with the help of the Amazons who come up to join them for *their* holidays, and a new tribe, the Eels. By now all the children are much older, and for the first time, too, Bridget is allowed to join them.

Although the make-believe adventures and one real one, when the three youngest are nearly cut off by the tide, make up the bulk of the book, the greatest interest is in a minor but to the young, most heart-searching question of loyalty to one's own gang in conflict with one's natural inclinations and desires.

The Big Six of the ninth book's title are the 2 D's, Tom Dudgeon and the Death and Glories, all of whom we met in *Coot Club*. This time they act as detectives and set out to discover who has been stealing from craft on the Broads, in order to clear the Death and Glories, who are suspected of being the culprits. This, of all the twelve books, is the nearest to the conventional 'rattling good yarn'; it is a most competent thriller and the Big Six put in some excellent (and scientific) detective work. It has a felicitous ending. In the course of their adventures, the Death and Glories catch a record pike. An elderly fisherman sees it newly stuffed and displayed in a glass case in the parlour of the 'Roaring Donkey'.

' "Are you the boys who caught that fish?" he asked.
"We didn't exactly . . ." began Joe.
"Poor lads," said the old man. "Poor lads. . . . So young and with nothing left to live for."
"Let's go and catch another," said Pete.'

* * *

The Great Northern Diver

'nests abroad . . . usually seen solitary.' *Sandars*

'nests in eastern North America, Greenland and Iceland, may nest in the Shetlands, as it is often round these islands all summer, but this has never been proved.' *Coward*

These quotations are the key to *Great Northern?*, the twelfth and last volume, which is as good as any of its predecessors, and some consider it better than any of them. If Arthur Ransome had to rest on his laurels, the publication of this book was surely the best of occasions.

The Swallows, the Amazons, and the 2 D's are sailing round the Hebrides with Uncle Jim. John must be fifteen or sixteen; Roger, eleven or twelve. It is the end of the holidays and they beach their borrowed boat to scrub her before returning her to her owner. Typically, there is a full-page plate of diagrams showing how a boat is supported on 'legs' when deliberately left high and dry by the receding tide. Dick, the naturalist of the party—trained on the Broads by the Coot Club!—makes his momentous discovery of a pair of Great Northern Divers nesting. All Dick wants to do is to take notes and to photograph them, but an unscrupulous professional egg-collector appears on the scene. It takes all the resourcefulness of the Swallows, the Amazons and the 2 D's to outwit him and at the same time to avoid capture themselves by the islanders who suspect that their curious manoeuvres on the island are part of some plan to poach their deer.

The final chase is as excitingly told as any incident in any of the books. Satisfactorily, it is Dick who saves the birds from being shot by the collector and Titty who finds the eggs that the villain had stolen from the nest. Together they put the eggs back in the nest, and the book ends with them watching the two Great Northern Divers return to sit on them.

' "Come on," said Titty. "Let's go and tell the others."

"Gosh! Oh gosh!" said Dick, almost as if he were Roger, and, blinking joyfully through his spectacles, pulled for the shore.'

VIII. Illustrations

All twelve of the books are very fully illustrated, with an average of twenty-six full-page plates (*Secret Water* has as many as forty-one), end-paper maps and numerous tail-pieces to the chapters. Today, the illustrations must be regarded by many people as an integral part of the saga, yet the first edition of *Swallows and Amazons* contained no pictures at all. The second edition carried end-paper maps by Stephen Spurrier, and illustrations by Clifford Webb. Stephen Spurrier's maps have a nice swashbuckling quality, and Clifford Webb is a fine decorative artist. Why, then, were all the books finally 'illustrated' by Arthur Ransome, who stated that he could not draw for toffee? What happened?

The answer is this: when Arthur Ransome wrote *Peter Duck* it struck him very forcibly that as the story was supposed to be written by the Swallows and Amazons themselves, it would add to the book's verisimilitude if they were also supposed to illustrate it. None of them (save, possibly, Titty?) could draw very well, so who better to make their pictures for them than the real author. A note at the beginning of *Peter Duck* states that all the children (even Roger) had a hand in the drawings, and is signed: 'Captain Nancy Blackett'.

Arthur Ransome decided that henceforth he would illustrate all his own books, and furthermore, that he would re-illustrate *Swallows and Amazons* and *Swallowdale*, the first edition of which had also been illustrated by Clifford Webb. The new edition of *Swallowdale* was announced as 'illustrated by the Author with help from Miss Nancy Blackett'; in *Winter Holiday* Arthur Ransome said, 'I have to thank Miss Nancy Blackett for much earnest work on the illustrations of this book'; and in *Pigeon Post* he wrote, 'As usual I have to thank Miss Nancy Blackett, whose drawing is improving hand over fist, for much help with the illustrations.'

Why did Arthur Ransome continue to illustrate all his books with Nancy's assistance? Was it a gimmick suggested by the publishers, or was Arthur Ransome secretly rather proud of his pictures? Were they his Achilles' heel? Neither answer is the right one. Arthur Ransome felt very strongly that the pictures are not, in the true sense, illustrations; they are really part of the text. He set out deliberately to give authenticity to the stories by drawing as he thought the children would draw. The drawings intentionally suggest the amateur to help the reader to trust in the reality of the story. They were, therefore, an extremely interesting innovation in the technique of illustrating—one must still use the word—children's books.

Whether or not Arthur Ransome's pictures do really make many children believe that the stories are true, they have one incontrovertible asset, they encourage the reader to identify himself or herself with a particular character. Not only are the figures in the drawings often shown at a distance, but they are frequently portrayed with, so to speak, their backs to the easel.

All this would make it sound as though none of Arthur Ransome's pictures had the merit of recognisable, critical portraiture. While I am prepared to accept Arthur Ransome's insistence on the value of bad drawing, I cannot agree that his drawings *are* so very bad. . . . Nor, I think, would Frank Eyre, for one of Arthur Ransome's drawings illus-

ARTHUR RANSOME

trates his *Twentieth Century Children's Books*—in most distinguished company. Arthur Ransome drew a number of entertaining and occasionally most moving pictures; his portraits of Uncle Jim/Captain Flint are among the most endearing, particularly as the profile is that of his portrayer; his pictures of boats, quays and islands have the feel of place; and his explanatory diagrams, whether they be of ship's rigging or of pigeons-ringing-bells-in-lofts, are as clear as blueprints. His secret is hard to guess, but part of it may lie in an almost oriental emphasis on relevant shape and detail combined with a disregard of irrelevant setting.

There is a curious likeness in one of the books, *Peter Duck*, between Arthur Ransome's drawings and those of another great children's author, Hugh Lofting. Hugh Lofting, Arthur Ransome thought, was a 'real' artist, and his aim was that of the usual illustrator. Nevertheless, some of Arthur Ransome's pictures in *Peter Duck* are startlingly like Lofting's. In the illustration, 'The Vipers Come Aboard', for instance, one instinctively looks for Jip's, or perhaps Gub-Gub's muzzle canted over the deckhouse, and one would not be in the least surprised to see Dab-Dab's anxious beak peering out of a porthole (how like Susan she is!) or Polynesia circling angrily round the rigging.

Still, one could make too much of this curious likeness; many of Arthur Ransome's other drawings are entirely different. And so, of course, was his intention.

Illustrators of those foreign editions that do not reproduce the originals have not for the most part been very successful, but one of the American editions of *Pigeon Post* is an outstanding exception; it is illustrated most attractively, not by an American artist but—oddly enough—by Mary Shepard, E. H. Shepard's daughter.

IX. Critics and Buyers

Swallows and Amazons was no immediate best seller either in its first, picture-less, or in its second, illustrated, edition. There were a lot of children's books on the market in 1930, and as Jonathan Cape said, the title was a sadly dull one. Besides, the author was known only as a journalist, critic and essayist, who liked fishing and sailing. And, if anyone cared to find out, he was already forty-six.

It was between two and three years before the book covered his £100 advance. *Swallowdale* did not sell particularly well either, at first, and it was not until December 1932 that the tide turned. On the 2nd of that month there appeared, in *The Times*, a most enthusiastic review of his third book, published just in time for Christmas, *Peter Duck*. That same month an equally appreciative one by Hugh Walpole appeared in the *Observer*.

This incidentally healed a breach between the two men, which had existed since 1916. They first knew each other in England in 1908 and met again in Russia, when Ransome, on the *Daily News*, contradicted a report by Walpole, who was running an Anglo-Russian bureau. Rupert Hart-Davis tells the story in his *Hugh Walpole*, but does not mention the sequel. Arthur Ransome wrote to Hugh Walpole after the *Observer* review and asked if it were 'an olive branch'. 'A twig', was the reply . . . and the two were friends again.

Ever since 1932, reviews have been uniformly, almost boringly, favourable. Reviewers from David Garnett and Rosamond Lehmann, M. E. Atkinson and Mary Treadgold to the provincial paraphrases of publishers' blurbs have been unhesitating and unstinting in praise. One can almost sympathise with the *Yorkshire Post* reviewer of *We Didn't Mean to Go to Sea* (hailed by David Garnett as 'the most exciting of the series' and by Eleanor Graham as 'one of the best books for the young I had ever read') when he or she writes: 'This year I was determined not to like Mr Ransome's book best . . . I surrender once more.'

Have there been no adverse criticisms? The only ones I have been able to discover have taxed Arthur Ransome with making his characters too nice—too kind and game and loyal, never cheating or squabbling. Of course no children behave so well for so long in real life, but what purpose is served by picking holes in heroes and heroines unless you do not find them credible without faults? And the chief characteristic of the Amazons, the Swallows, the 2 D's, the Death and Glories and the Eels, is that they are supremely credible and memorable. The truth is not that they have no faults but that Arthur Ransome legitimately prefers to show them to us at their nicest, which is when they are happiest and at their most interesting.

The most valuable review of Arthur Ransome's work is perhaps the long article that was published in the *Times Literary Supplement* of June 16, 1950, under the heading 'A Contemporary Classic'. The writer concentrates on the characters rather than the plots. To my mind it is therefore all the more surprising that he should wind up by acclaiming *Peter Duck* as 'perhaps the high-water mark'. To make amends for my admittedly rather summary and certainly prejudiced dismissal of the book, I should, I think, quote this: 'Here is something for every taste mixed together in an irresistible hotch-potch of humour and fantasy, realism and romance.' Another—and to the best of my knowledge the only other—detailed study of Arthur Ransome is by the

Canadian Children's Librarian, Lillian H. Smith, in *The Unreluctant Years* (American Library Association, 1953). She makes an interesting analysis of *Great Northern?* and draws attention to the remarkable quality of what she finds to be Arthur Ransome's three quite distinct styles. First, she points out, there is scientific detail, described with the 'precise minuteness and the practical language of Defoe'; then there is his dialogue, 'natural and unassuming', and finally his description of action and setting. I would agree with her evaluation of Arthur Ransome's style, but cannot see that its character changes so noticeably according to his subject matter. Colloquial simplicity and a marked economy of words are its hallmarks and can be seen, I think, even in the short extracts quoted in this monograph. He never wastes words in achieving his effect, whether it be humorous, dramatic or didactic, and it is due to this that he can slip from description to narrative to dialogue so easily and naturally.

Arthur Ransome's literary success has been complete, but what of his commercial success? In 1952 the University of Leeds—where his father had been Professor of History—conferred on him the degree of Doctor of Letters, and he was awarded a C.B.E. in the New Year Honours of 1953, but have his books sold as phenomenally as those of far lesser children's writers? His publishers are reticent about exact figures, but they admit that in 1958 *Swallows and Amazons* alone had sold over 210,000 copies.

This refers, of course, only to the English edition. Arthur Ransome's books have long been published in the United States, by Lippincott and Macmillan, and they have been welcomed by American children's librarians. What is more surprising, they have proved and are still proving successful in a large number of non-English-speaking countries, and have been translated into twelve foreign languages: Czech, French, Swedish, German, Norwegian, Danish, Dutch, Icelandic, Finnish, Hungarian, Polish, and Spanish.

It would be entertaining to study the variations in the different editions. In the French version of *Swallows and Amazons*, for instance, when the children are clearing up for the night on Wild Cat Island, all their activities are faithfully recorded with the exception of their brewing a final cup of tea! National and even religious feeling has demanded other alterations, not necessarily acceptable to the author. Arthur Ransome did put his foot down when one continental publisher begged him to let the Walkers and Blacketts say their prayers before they went to sleep.

It was not until 1962 that a paperback edition of *Swallows and Amazons* appeared under the Puffin imprint. Three more, *Swallowdale*, *Winter Holiday* and *Peter Duck*, are now available in a Puffin edition; the other eight books are to be published in paperback in 1969 and 1970. There has also been a limited edition of *Swallows and Amazons*. The BBC has broadcast dramatised versions of the stories on sound radio, and several of them were brilliantly read aloud by Derek McCulloch. A film of *Swallows and Amazons* was made by BBC Television in 1963.

x. Children and the Writer

Although most children's books would not sell if children did not like them, not all sales can be accounted for by the number of appreciative juvenile readers. Parents and librarians are the main buyers, which may account for the continuance in print of dust-dull 'classics' that are considered salutary or at least safe. How can one gauge children's reactions to Arthur Ransome's books? There is no single certain method, but it is of some interest and value to look at the results of a competition held by Jonathan Cape in 1941. While the bombs began to fall on London, children were asked to write 250 words on their favourite Ransome. *Missee Lee* had only just been published, while *The Picts and the Martyrs* and *Great Northern?* were yet to be written. There were two 'winners', a girl of nine, who plumped for *Missee Lee* (which smacks of opportunism), and a boy of eight and a half who chose *We Didn't Mean to Go to Sea*. This proves precisely nothing, but what is important is Mary Treadgold's report. 'Out of all the entries', she wrote in Cape's *Now and Then*, 'one point emerged—and that was that there was no consensus of opinion.' Evidently, children might agree with the author that the books are all volumes of the same work.

Both boys and girls have now been reading Arthur Ransome for a third of a century. The Swallows and the Amazons are real to millions of people all over the world, and the Lake District, at least that part that is not William Wordsworth's, has become as much Ransome Country as Sussex is Kipling's, Belloc's or Sheila Kaye-Smith's and

Dorset is Thomas Hardy's. Elinor Saltus of Arizona University was prevailed upon by her son to make a pilgrimage to meet Arthur Ransome in his own territory. In *Elementary English*, she relates how he told her that when he returned to Peel/Wild Cat Island some years after the publication of *Swallows and Amazons*, he found that actual navigation marks had been placed on the rocks to guide boats into the hidden harbour. One other thing he told her shows the effect of the books on children. A little girl wrote to him from Africa to say that she knew he was writing about her own country because she could show him the lake near her home with every spot he mentioned located on it.

What sort of children are Ransome enthusiasts? Are they, as one would expect, predominantly middle-class? The immense sales would make one query this, even if Arthur Ransome himself did not violently contradict the notion, and produce letters from working-class schools in northern mining districts showing that whole classes of boys who could never afford the Walkers' type of holiday were fascinated by the books.

As is the case with most authors, two or three decades after reaching the peak of their popularity, Arthur Ransome may well be read less and less for a while. But his popularity will return and return for good, because his basic stories are universal and even on the surface they do not date. One reason is that his dialogue though always colloquial is never spattered with contemporary slang.

In general the people who do not like Ransome's books are found to be those who do not share his hobbies and interests and who do not enjoy doing things for themselves. It is for this reason that many parents are mystified by the fascination the books exert over their children. The other most common cause for complaint is that the stories are too technical. And one can understand this point of view if anyone picking up *Swallows and Amazons* for the first time should find, as I did, the book opening at page 29.

'Susan had got the sail ready. On the gaff there was a strop (which is really a loop), that hooked on a hook on one side of an iron ring called the traveller, because it moved up and down the mast. The halyard ran from the traveller up to the top of the mast, through a sheave . . .'

The fact that Arthur Ransome thereupon explains what a sheave is would be small comfort to those not vitally interested.

When one is initiated into the books, and even if one is a ten-thumbed landlubber, there is nothing more delightful than his obsession with the workings of things, and his passion for passing on odd lore. During the course of reading the saga one can learn how to skin a rabbit, tickle a trout, catch, clean and smoke eels, use semaphore, assay copper, keep milk cool, lay patterns, burn charcoal, make a map and take flashlight photographs.

But these are incidental delights. What will remain will be the children, as secure of a place in literature as Jim Hawkins or the Bastables, Kay Harker or the Ruggles. As Marcus Crouch has written,* they are 'the most unself-conscious of all fictional children. Each is a highly individual person, carefully observed; each grows and develops through contact with the others and with circumstance.'

How did Arthur Ransome do it? Oddly enough, by enjoying himself—after nearly thirty years' training in writing what pleased and amused him far less. In 1937 he wrote a letter to the *Junior Bookshelf* at the request of the editor, who wanted to know 'how he did it'. His answer was to

* *Chosen for Children*, Library Association, 1957.

quote the one author he loved most as a child, Robert Louis Stevenson,

'It's awful fun, boys' stories; you just indulge the pleasure of your heart . . .'

'That, it seems to me, is the secret,' was Arthur Ransome's comment. 'You write not *for* children but for yourself, and if, by good fortune, children enjoy what you enjoy, why then you are a writer of children's books. . . . No special credit to you, but simply thumping good luck.'

To my belief this was not the amiable white lie of a nice man refusing to discuss the agony of writing what children read with careless ease. It was the honest statement of a very great craftsman who only cared about what he made—and who made only what he truly cared about.

BIBLIOGRAPHY

Bibliography

I. CHECK LIST

The Souls of the Streets and Other Little Papers, 1904
The Stone Lady, Ten Little Papers and Two Mad Stories, 1905
Highways and Byways in Fairyland, [1906]
The Child's Book of the Seasons, 1906
Things in Our Garden, 1906
Pond and Stream, 1906
Bohemia in London, 1907
A History of Story-Telling, 1909
Edgar Allan Poe, 1910
The Hoofmarks of the Faun, 1911
Oscar Wilde, 1912
Portraits and Speculations, 1913
The Elixir of Life, 1915
Old Peter's Russian Tales, 1916
Aladdin and His Wonderful Lamp in Rhyme, [1919]
Six Weeks in Russia in 1919, 1919
The Soldier and Death, 1920
The Crisis in Russia, 1921
The Chinese Puzzle, 1927
Rod and Line, 1929
'Racundra's' First Cruise, 1923
Swallows and Amazons, 1930. Illustrated edition, 1931. Edition
    with A.R.'s own illustrations, 1938. Limited edition, 1958.
    Paperback edition, 1962
Swallowdale, 1931. Edition illustrated by A. R., 1938. Paperback
    edition, 1968
Peter Duck, 1932. Paperback edition, 1968
Winter Holiday, 1933. Paperback edition, 1968
Coot Club, 1934
Pigeon Post, 1936

* Out of print.

63

We Didn't Mean to Go to Sea, 1937
Secret Water, 1939
The Big Six, 1940
Missee Lee, 1941
The Picts and the Martyrs, 1943
Great Northern?, 1947
Fishing, 1955
Mainly about Fishing, 1959

II. BOOKS EDITED,

TRANSLATED OR WITH CONTRIBUTIONS BY

ARTHUR RANSOME

[N.B. This list is by no means exhaustive]

THE WORLD'S STORY-TELLERS

A series under the general editorship of Arthur Ransome,
each book with an introduction by him

Théophile Gautier, 1908
Ernst T. A. Hoffman, 1908
Edgar Allan Poe, 1908
Prosper Mérimée, 1908
Nathaniel Hawthorne, 1908
Honoré de Balzac, 1909
François R. de Chateaubriand, 1909
The Essayists, 1909
M. de Cervantes, 1909
Gustave Flaubert, 1909
Alphonse Daudet and François Coppée, 1909

The Book of Friendship. Edited by Arthur Ransome, [1909]
A Night in the Luxembourg, by Rémy de Gourmont, 1912. Translated, with a preface and appendix, by Arthur Ransome
The Book of Love, [1910]. Edited by Arthur Ransome
A Week, by Y. N. Libedinsky, 1923. Translated by Arthur Ransome
Down Channel, by R. T. MacMullen, 1931. Introduction by Arthur Ransome

BIBLIOGRAPHY

The Cruise of the 'Teddy', by Erling Tambs, 1933. Introduction by Arthur Ransome

The Far-Distant Oxus, by Katherine Hull and Pamela Whitlock, 1937. Foreword by Arthur Ransome

Sailing Alone Around the World, by Joshua Slocum, 1948. Introduction by Arthur Ransome

The Falcon on the Baltic, by E. F. Knight, 1951. Introduction by Arthur Ransome

The Cruise of the 'Alerte', by E. F. Knight, 1952. Introduction by Arthur Ransome

The Cruise of the 'Kate', by E. E. Middleton, 1953. Introduction by Arthur Ransome

The Voyage Alone in the Yawl 'Rob Roy', by John MacGregor, 1954. Introduction by Arthur Ransome

Rudyard Kipling

ROSEMARY SUTCLIFF

CONTENTS

1. Early Days

In the High and Far Off days when the Indian Mutiny was only seven years past and the Indian Empire only seven years old, a son was born to John Lockwood Kipling, Principal of the new School of Art in Bombay. He was a first child, and his parents called him Rudyard after the lake beside which they had done most of their courting.

Rudyard Kipling's first few years were lived in a bungalow in the compound of the School of Art, uncomfortably near to the Towers of Silence on which the Parsees exposed their dead to the vultures—so uncomfortably near that unconsidered bits of dead Parsee were constantly falling into the garden. The ayah who looked after his little sister was a Goanese Roman Catholic, and used often to take him to the chapel of her faith. Meeta, the bearer, was a Hindu, and took him just as often to the temple of Shiva; and he went to either place of worship with equal willingness. Indeed, all his life he never followed completely the teachings of any one faith, and perhaps his free thinking had its beginnings in this richly varied religious upbringing of his earliest years.

For Service families, or families whose business keeps them in hot countries, there are nearly always agonising partings to be faced as the children grow older, and when Rudyard was five and his little sister not yet three, there was a trip to England from which the parents returned alone, leaving the children as paying guests in the house of a retired naval officer at Southsea. Why they were left to the care of strangers is a mystery. One of Mrs Kipling's sisters was married to a rich ironmaster, Alfred Baldwin, another—

71

the adored Aunt Georgie—to Burne-Jones, and the third to Sir Edward Poynter, afterwards President of the Royal Academy. They all had children and they were devoted sisters, and the obvious thing would have seemed to be for one of them to take Rudyard and Trix.

The six years that he spent in Southsea were the most wretched of Kipling's whole life, and he emerged from them having used up his whole supply of hate on the mistress of the house (whom he writes of in his autobiography as 'The Woman'), so that he was never able to feel a really full-blooded hate for anyone else. Trix, the little sister, did well enough in the 'House of Desolation'; it was only Rudyard who, for some unknown reason, came in for the full force of The Woman's zeal for the rooting out of sin, and him she terrified with Hell Fire and sought to reform with punishments and persecutions through all those six years.

But in each year there was one shining month which he and Trix spent with Aunt Georgie, a month during which they lived, so far as the nursery of those days could live, in the society of the adult world, of men like Burne-Jones and William Morris: William Morris, who, finding the aunt and uncle out one day when he called, came up to the schoolroom, and, seated creakingly majestic on the ancient rocking-horse, regaled its inhabitants with the story-outline of the Saga of Burnt Njal.

The one other shining thing in those dark years was that at some point in them the child Rudyard discovered what reading was about. When he could read, a friend of The Woman's gave him a little purple book called *The Hope of the Katzikopfs*. It was of severely moral tone, but it contained verses that began 'Farewell Rewards and Fairies', from which seed came flower and fruit at a later date.

The end of the Southsea period came when the small boy's

eyes went wrong. He was found to be half blind and on the
edge of some kind of breakdown; his mother returned from
India unexpectedly, and when she came to his bedside and
bent to kiss him goodnight, he flung up his arm to ward off
the blow he had grown to expect. That was the end of The
Woman, and the beginning of five years at the United
Service College, at Westward Ho! on the North Devon
coast.

Cormell Price, the headmaster, was a personal friend of
the Kiplings, which made the choice an obvious one, and
this time all went well. The College had been started only a
few years before by a handful of Service officers wanting a
cheap but sound education for their sons, but though it was
founded by Service officers and most of its boys went into
one or other of the Services in their turn, anything less like
a military academy could scarcely be imagined. There were
no parades, no uniforms, no bands or flags—indeed for the
school's opinion of such things one has only to read the
chapter in *Stalky & Co.* which deals with the Jelly-bellied
Flag-flapper. The school buildings had been converted from
a terrace of twelve bleak lodging houses; the food 'would
have provoked a mutiny in Dartmoor today'; it was a hard
school, but most of its boys remembered it afterwards with
love. Certainly Kipling did.

Into the midst of the United Service College he burst at
the age of not quite twelve, a small boy with an enormous
smile, a pair of bright blue eyes behind very thick spectacles
which immediately gained him the name of Gig-lamps, and
already the first faint foreshadowing of a moustache. On
his very first day he made common cause with a bony-faced
Irish boy, George Beresford by name, and before his first
year was out, the two were joined by 'Stalky' Dunsterville.
Thereafter, the three went up the school together, frequently

at war amongst themselves, but presenting a united and extremely formidable front to the rest of the world.

They were to be in later years the Beetle, MacTurk and Stalky of *Stalky & Co.*, a book which abounds in portraits and semi-portraits.

II. The Young Writer

At the end of the 1882 summer term the schoolboy triumvirate broke up, and the future took them their separate ways; Dunsterville to be a soldier, Beresford a civil engineer, Kipling at the age of sixteen and three-quarters, to sail for India and a job as assistant editor of the *Civil and Military Gazette*, published in Lahore.

His father and mother had lately moved to Lahore from Bombay, and John Lockwood Kipling was now Principal of the School of Art and Curator of the Museum, which stood, just as described in *Kim*, beside the Mall running from the European quarter to the old native city. So young Kipling lived with his parents, but had his own room, his own servant, his own horse and dog-cart, and (glory of glories!) his own office-box to take to work every morning. And when a year or so later Trix came out to join them, the whole family were united again.

The job of assistant editor meant in fact that young Kipling was 'fifty per cent of the editorial staff' and worked hours accordingly, ten to fifteen of them a day. But somehow, especially when his family had gone up to the hills for the hot weather, where he could only follow them for a month out of the three or four that they would be away, he found time to rediscover India. Chiefly at night, the dark hot fever-smelling nights when nobody could sleep and much of the life of Lahore went on in the streets or on the roof tops, he would explore the ancient Muslim city crouched under the grim square fortress reeking of many ghosts, from which Ranjit Singh, the Lion of the Punjab, had ruled his short-lived Sikh kingdom. And these night-time prowlings, as well as the odder side of his newspaper work, brought him many unusual friends. One, a certain Pathan horse dealer named Mahbub Ali, later to become familiar to readers of *Kim*, a man of 'indescribable filth but magnificent mien and features', brought him news of Central Asia beyond the Khyber Pass. He also got to know both officers and men of the British Infantry companies which now garrisoned the old Sikh fort; and at the Lahore Club he sat among representatives of the Army, Education, Canals, Forestry, Engineering, Irrigation, Railways, Medicine and Law, all talking in great detail their own particular brand of 'shop'. And all these things and people played a part in making him the kind of writer that he afterwards became.

Three years after he came out from England, he began writing short stories for the *Civil and Military Gazette*, under the collective title of *Plain Tales from the Hills*, which were used as and when extra material was needed. And the thing had begun. In 1887 he was transferred to the staff of the *Pioneer* at Allahabad, where, stimulated by the change, he promptly wrote the horrifyingly precocious *Story of the Gadsbys*. His new job entailed a good deal of travelling about Northern India in search of copy, including a visit to the Rajput States of the Indian Desert, which filled his notebooks with local colour. And on this trip a few hours spent in the abandoned city of Amber furnished him with the 'Cold Lairs' of the *Jungle Books*.

But the Indian phase of Kipling's life was closing and another opening to him, as his writing became better known. By the end of 1889 he was in London again; and in London, like Lord Byron before him, he woke up one morning to find himself famous. His *Ballad of East and West*, that most often quoted and misquoted of all his works, was published in November, and from then on, everything he wrote was eagerly sought after. He began to meet all the great literary figures of the day; he began to make so much money that soon he had a whole thousand pounds in the bank, and got his beloved family home on a short visit to share his astonished delight. At that time also he met Walcott Balestier, a young American agent for a New York firm of publishers, and struck up a devoted friendship with him, which resulted, among other things, in their combining to write *The Naulahka*.

This friendship led also to a meeting with Balestier's sister Carrie; and long before *The Naulahka* was published, the two of them had reached 'an understanding'. But there was still no formal engagement when Kipling set off on a voyage that was intended to take him round the world and return him for a while to his own folk in Lahore. After some time in South Africa, Australia and New Zealand, he reached Lahore just before Christmas 1891, but hardly had he done so when he received word from Carrie that Walcott was dead. He left at once, and was back in England a fortnight later. He never saw India again.

Within a week, he and Carrie were married by special licence; Carrie, according to eye witness reports, in 'a brown woollen dress with buttons all down the front'. Most of Kipling's friends, and certainly his mother, were more than doubtful of how this marriage to a clever, dominating and rather hard woman three years older than himself was going to work out, but it worked out, on the whole, very happily. After a honeymoon trip dramatically cut short by an unforeseen failure of funds, they settled down in a farm cottage near the little town of Brattleborough in Vermont, which was Carrie's home ground. And there, in late autumn of 1892, with snow piled to the windowsills and Carrie in process of having a baby, Kipling wrote a boy-and-wolf story called *Mowgli's Brothers*.

III. Best Beloved

The original impulse for *Mowgli's Brothers* was derived, so say both Kipling and Rider Haggard, from a scene in Haggard's *Nada the Lily*, in which Umslopogaas, the Zulu hero, runs with a wolf pack; but the whole process of thought leading on from that impulse to become the *Jungle Books* with their hero swinging between two worlds, and their strange ethical concept, the Law of the Jungle, is all Kipling's own. In this one, alone of all his books, the topography and local colour are second-hand, for the background of the Mowgli stories is along the banks of the Waingunga River in the Seonee district, a part of Central India which he had never visited. He worked, in that little snowbound New England cottage, from descriptions and photographs sent to him four years earlier by some friends; just as he took his wild animals and Indian lore from his father's knowledge of all things Indian and from Sterndale's *Mammalia of India*. The wonderful thing is that one would never guess it.

The Jungle Book was finished at the tail end of the year, about the time that little Josephine, her father's Best Beloved, came into the world; *The Second Jungle Book* two and a half years later. It seems worth noticing that out of Kipling's long writing life of more than fifty years, all his stories for children, and the stories that, though not specifically written for children are read and loved by them, were written in the seventeen or eighteen years between the time when his first child was on the way and the time when his last child was too old to have stories written for him any more.

In 1894 when *The Second Jungle Book* was still being

78

written, there was a visit to England, and to Kipling's parents, who had by now retired and were living in the little Wiltshire village of Tisbury. In the Tisbury cottage, under his father's eye (John Lockwood was always his son's severest as well as favourite critic) the most delicate of all the stories of the *Jungle Books*, not a Mowgli story at all, but the exquisite *Miracle of Purun Bhagat* was written.

When the family returned to Vermont, it was to a big newly-built timber house of their own, 'The Naulahka', and there, in 1896, Elsie was born. By then the idea for *Kim* was stirring in Kipling's mind, but refused to come down out of the void and take shape, and shortly after visits from the local doctor to Carrie and the new baby turned his creative energies for the time being into another channel. Dr Conland had been to sea in his youth, and would sit, after his official visits, yarning about his young days and the fishermen of the Grand Banks; from which yarns grew a book called *Captains Courageous*. That book took them, as Kipling writes in his autobiography,

'to the shore front, and the old T wharf of Boston Harbour, and to queer meals in sailors' eating houses, where he renewed his youth among ex-shipmates and their kin. We assisted hospitable tug-masters to help three- and four-stick schooners of Pochahontas coal all round the harbour; we boarded every craft that looked as if she might be useful, and we delighted ourselves to the limit of delight.'

But in spite of the children and the books growing up in it, 'The Naulahka' remained only a house and never became a home; there was trouble with Carrie's younger brother who lived close by, and small-town life, where all things political were linked with anti-British feeling, was not the life for Kipling, not the standpoint from which he could write. So once again an old phase ended and a new one began.

They arrived in England at summer's end of 1896, and took a house at Torquay. There, after Sir George Robertson, the hero of the siege of Chitral, had been to them on a visit, and his thoughts were full of Frontier fighting, Kipling wrote *Slaves of the Lamp* which in the end made the final episode of *Stalky & Co.* and having begun at the end, added the earlier chapters from time to time over the next three years. But neither he nor Carrie was ever happy at 'Rock House', and after eight months they fled from Torquay to Rottingdean, a little half-lost downland village in those days, where the Burne-Jones Aunt and Uncle and the Baldwin Cousin (afterwards Prime Minister) had their holiday houses. The Kiplings' son, John, was born in the Burne-Jones' house on a summer night in 1899, and soon after they rented 'The Elms' across the village green, which was to be their home for five years.

Meanwhile *Kim* had begun to stir again, more insistently this time, and that autumn Kipling took his idea for a story about the son of an Irish soldier plunged into the drifting life of wayfaring India up to Tisbury to be 'smoked over' with his father; and a little later, back at 'The Elms', he began telling the *Just So Stories* to Josephine, for whom all the earlier ones were written. But his time for telling stories to Josephine, his Best Beloved, was to be tragically short. Early 1900 brought an unexpected business trip to the U.S.A. on which Carrie insisted on taking the three children. All three caught whooping cough on arrival in New York, and Kipling himself went down with pneumonia, leaving Carrie to cope with all of them in a New York hotel. Josephine followed her father into pneumonia, and had not his strength to fight it. On March 6th, just as he came out of danger, the child died; and for her parents—certainly for her father—life was never quite the same again.

IV. The Fairy Ring

A few weeks after Josephine's death, the Kiplings returned to 'The Elms', and that autumn *Stalky & Co.* was published amid a storm of divided opinion. Kipling was now at the height of his fame, and trippers from Brighton had begun to discover the house where he lived; a house, moreover, where every corner, every shadowy hiding-place under the garden bushes, was charged with the memory of a little fair-haired girl. Rottingdean had lost its happiness and its charm.

The Boer War came, and swept Kipling and his wife off to South Africa, where there was plenty waiting for him to do. But that, as he might have said himself, is another story. Back at Rottingdean once more for a few months in the summer of 1901, he finished *Kim*, having carried it, in one way or another, for seven years.

South Africa had given them many new friends, including Cecil Rhodes, and from 1901 to 1908, the family's every winter was spent at their own cottage 'The Woolsack', built for them close to Rhodes's own house, 'Groote Schuur'. At 'The Woolsack' Kipling took up again the long laid aside *Just So Stories*, to tell to the other children, now that the child they had been made for was gone. And there he completed the book with *The Cat that Walked by Himself* and *The Butterfly that Stamped*.

But meanwhile, during the English half of the year, the Kiplings were carrying out a systematic all-over-Sussex search for the House of the Perfect Eaves. A search which ended at last when they came, driving a 'Victoria hooded, carriage sprung, carriage braked, single cylinder, belt driven, fixed ignition' Lanchester down an enlarged rabbit hole of a lane, and found at the bottom of it, 'Bateman's'.

Kipling describes 'Bateman's' as grey; he should know the colour of the house, for it was his home for more than thirty years, but to my mind it is warmer than grey, almost tawny. A warm and welcoming house of many gables and more chimneys, with the date 1634 over the door, and a dovecot like a small fortress at the back; and over all and through all, an atmosphere, gentle and quiet, made up of many layers of time. Not only the house, but the whole valley, was gloriously rich in the past of Sussex; at the bottom of a newly sunk well they turned up the bronze cheek-piece of a Roman bridle. Dredging out a choked pond produced two Elizabethan 'Sealed Quarts' and a Neolithic axehead. On the fringe of 'Bateman's' land, in a little lost valley,

'stood the long overgrown slag heap of a most ancient forge, supposed to have been worked by the Phoenicians and Romans, and since then, uninterruptedly till the middle of the eighteenth century. The bracken and rush-patches still hid stray pigs of iron, and if one scratched a few inches through the rabbit-shaven turf, one came on the narrow mule-track of peacock-hued furnace-slag laid down in Elizabeth's day. The ghost of a road climbed up out of this dead arena, and crossed our fields, where it was known as "The Gunway" and popularly connected with Armada times. Every foot of that little corner was alive with ghosts and shadows.'

Every foot of it, too, must have been alive for Kipling with the raw material of creative magic. For some time the idea of a book of stories from English history had been stirring in his mind, and he had taken it, as usual, to 'smoke over' with his father. And then in their third October at 'Bateman's', Elsie and John decided to perform a 'Play of Puck and Titania', for which their father asked a friend in

London to get them a paper donkey's head for Bottom. For stage they had a fairy ring beside the brook, at the foot of the grassy spur which they had christened 'Pook's Hill'. (There are several Pook's Hills in Sussex, but that, until the Kiplings came, does not seem to have been one of them.) And so both the setting and the mechanics of magic for *Puck of Pook's Hill* presented itself. By the following January Kipling was hard at work, and *Puck*, together with *Rewards and Fairies*, took up a large part of his attention for the next five years. The first tale in his mind, based on a suggestion from a cousin, was about a Roman centurion called Parnesius, but the Norman and Saxon stories of Sir Richard Dalyngridge materialised first, and Parnesius came later, walking out of the little wood above the Phoenician forge. The rest followed in due order. *Puck of Pook's Hill* was published in 1906, and then came a pause while the writer experimented. He tried and rejected stories about Dr Johnson, Daniel Defoe and King Arthur; but at last the eleven stories and their attendant poems which go to make up *Rewards and Fairies* were published in 1910.

The following year, when C. R. L. Fletcher's *History of England* was published, it contained songs of Kipling's that are of the same stream as those of *Puck* and *Rewards*.

Those were the last words that Kipling ever wrote for children.

And so, from the point of view of this sketch, the story ends. But to round off neatly and in seemly fashion, in the manner of the nineteenth-century novels: John was killed at Loos in his eighteenth year; Elsie married in 1924, and the final end of the story came when Rudyard Kipling died at the age of seventy, only a day or so before his close friend King George V, and was buried in the Poets' Corner in Westminster Abbey, on January 22nd, 1936.

v. A Choice of Books

I have begun this sketch of Kipling as a writer for children with an outline of his life, because in his case, even more than most of the brotherhood, the life and the writings are bound together. Every book, every short story, has its origin in his background or the events and circumstances of his life. They came of his Indian experiences, they grew from yarnings over a pipe with a Vermont country doctor, they were written because he went to a particular school, and because he had much-loved children to tell them to.

I have left out a very great deal because it had not to do with the children's writer; journeyings to the uttermost ends of the earth, world events through which he moved and on which so many of his greatest poems were comments, the many honours that he refused and the few that he accepted. I have named scarcely any of his books, other than those written for children. I have not even mentioned *Recessional*. But all these are to be found elsewhere. A good and detailed biography is *Rudyard Kipling, his Life and Work* by Professor Charles Carrington, published by Macmillan in 1955. A magnificent study of his writing is *The Art of Rudyard Kipling* by Dr J. M. S. Tompkins, published by Methuen in 1959 and *Kipling and the Children* by Roger Lancelyn Green, published by Elek Books Ltd in 1965, gives the complete picture, which in this short study I have sketched in outline. All three of these might well be read by those who feel like it, in conjunction with Kipling's own posthumously published autobiography, *Something of Myself*.

So far the task has been simple enough; the straightforward chronicling of facts. But the next stage is not so easy.

My first difficulty has been to decide just what, out of all Kipling's works, to include among his books for children. The first half-dozen, of course, are obvious: *Stalky* and the *Just So Stories*, both *Puck* books and both *Jungle Books*. After that, *Kim* and *Captains Courageous*. These two must certainly be included, although they were not specifically written for children. But having opened the ranks to them, where to draw the line? There are magnificent stories within the capacity of an intelligent twelve- or thirteen-year-old in most of the volumes of short stories, but they are such a wondrously mixed bag that I do not think I would encourage a child to wander among them unsupervised, though I would certainly not prevent him from doing so if he really wanted to. Myself, I fell upon *Many Inventions* in my twelfth year, and revelled in it. It contains one tale, *In the Rukh*, which is simply another Mowgli story, though it was never included in the *Jungle Books*; but it contains also a hideous tragedy called *Love o' Women*, which I read and re-read with the fascinated horror of half understanding, and which filled me with a terror of venereal disease (which I never had the sense to confide to anybody) through all my growing-up years.

So—Kipling's volumes of short stories are for the odd child here and there, but I shall not include them now; nor his one other full-length novel, *The Light that Failed*. A girl of sixteen or so may weep buckets over it, but that counts as grown-up reading. And nor shall I include '*Thy Servant, a Dog*' because I feel very strongly that it is unworthy of its writer. It is full of false sentiment, and the appalling whimsy of Boots' basic English might well put a child off the rest of Kipling for ever.

My choice then is the first and second *Jungle Books*, *Captains Courageous*, *Stalky & Co.*, *Kim*, the *Just So Stories*, *Puck of Pook's Hill* and *Rewards and Fairies*.

vi. Two Worlds

The *Jungle Books* step first upon the scene, not because they were the first to be written (I am not going to attempt to be chronological, I am simply going to arrange the books in the order in which they seem to fit most happily together), but because they were my own first introduction to Kipling. I was not more than five or six at the time, but I possessed a mother who read aloud most beautifully, and found great joy in doing it, and so from the first, I was able to enjoy books far in advance of those I could have coped with myself. From our earliest acquaintance I loved the Mowgli stories with a rather special love, not necessarily stronger, but different in kind from the love I had for any other book. I loved them for their strangeness, their 'otherness' which was somehow kept from ever getting out of bounds or becoming frightening by the familiar pattern of Mowgli's own relationships, for instance with the cosy close-drawn family life of Father and Mother Wolf and the four cubs. My feeling for the stories has of course changed with the years, without weakening; and in a way the stories themselves seem to have changed, too, for like nearly all the really great children's books, they are written on many levels, and for me they have become a following-out of divided life and divided loyalties, the unbearable choice that has to be made and has to be borne. Now also, having come to be a writer myself, I can stand back a little and appreciate, amongst sundry other matters, the superb craftsmanship that has gone into creating the Jungle Folk, each one a perfectly rounded individual (save of course for the Monkey

People, whose whole essence is that they are not individuals at all, but merely a gibbering mob) and each one perfectly within the bounds of his own animal nature. These are not human beings in animal skins, as even *Black Beauty*, another love of my childhood, tends to be; nothing so un-dignified. They are animals lordly in their own right, with the innate dignity of the wild animal who has never been taught to ride a bicycle in a circus.

I realised, of course, precisely nothing of all that when I was five, but I accepted the Jungle Dwellers as dear and deeply satisfying friends, and they were so real to me, especially Bagheera with the voice as soft as wild honey dripping from a tree, that remembering those early readings with my mother, I can still recapture the physical sensation of the living, sensuous, velvet-over-fire-and-steel-springs warmth of his skin, as though I had in actual fact once been on stroking terms with a black panther. I was aware also of Kipling's extraordinary power of getting under the skin of man or beast, time or place or situation, which has seemed to me ever since to be one of his greatest gifts; and I remember trying to explain to my mother what I felt about this: 'Well you see, other people write about things from the outside in, but Kipling writes about them from the inside out.' And therein lies a world of difference.

As a child I loved *The Jungle Book* best, because I knew that all would go well with the people I loved in it; I knew that even when Mowgli was turned out of the pack, he would come back to spread Shere Khan's hide on the Council Rock. But as soon as *The Second Jungle Book* was begun (my mother and I always read straight through from one to the other) I began to smell desolation in store, and even across that most wonderful story of *The King's Ankus* lay the shadow of *Red Dog* and *The Spring Running*. I could scarcely bear to listen to either of those two stories; the first battered me and tore at my heart strings with the tremendous sorrows of tragic saga, the second made my whole world ache with griefs and longings that I could not yet understand. But I am inclined to think that it does a child no harm to have its heart wrung occasionally. It broadens the mind and deepens the compassion.

At any mention of the *Jungle Books*, it is always the Mowgli stories that spring to mind; but there are of course many other stories beside. In my young days I particularly loved those of *Rikki-Tikki-Tavy* and *The White Seal* (why did the story of Kotik always seem so sad? When one comes to think of it, it had a perfectly good happy ending) which now I would exchange, both of them together, for that most lovely and strong and fragile story, *The Miracle of Purun Baghat*, which in those days was beyond my reach, as I think it would be beyond the reach of most children. But what is beyond his reach, the child will come back and reach up for again, when once his imagination has been captured; and there is in the *Jungle Books* plenty to catch at the imagination.

* * *

'The lama, very straight and erect, the deep folds of his yellow clothing slashed with black in the light of the *parao* fires precisely as a knotted tree trunk is slashed with the shadows of the long sun, addressed a tinsel and lacquered *ruth* (oxcart) which burned like a many coloured jewel in the same uncertain light. The patterns on the gold-worked curtain ran up and down, melting and re-forming as the folds shook and quivered in the night wind; and when the talk grew more earnest the jewelled forefinger snapped out little sparks of light between the embroideries. Behind the cart was a wall of uncertain darkness speckled with little flames and alive with half-caught forms and faces and shadows.'

I have given the quotation at length, because it expresses so perfectly two of the aspects of *Kim*. Firstly the preoccupation with light. Kipling could never visualise any incident without its attendant light and weather, season of the year and time of day; and in *Kim*, I think more than any other of his books, one is constantly aware of changing light; the wash of light across the tawny grass of a hill-side, the chill grey light of dawn over waking camp or railway siding, the smoky flare of torches.

Secondly, the sense of crowding riches—riches so vast that they overflowed in all directions and much could not be used at all, though one senses them behind the rest, a shifting background 'speckled with little flames and alive with half-caught forms and faces and shadows'. Kipling himself, describing the process of smoking over the book with his father, writes:

'Under our united tobacco it grew like the Djinn released from the brass bottle, and the more we explored its possibilities the more opulence of detail did we discover. I do not know what proportion of an iceberg is below the waterline, but *Kim*, as it finally appeared, was about one tenth of what the first lavish specification called for.'

And that is exactly the impression that the reader gets.

Superficially *Kim* is a spy story, and such plot as it has concerns a boy's education to be a Secret Service agent. But the plot is little more than a thread on which to string jewels as fascinating and curious as any in the shop of Lurgan Sahib, 'The Healer of Sick Pearls'. This is why the magnificent and vastly expensive film made from the book some years ago was merely the husk, though a colourful and entertaining husk, with all the peculiar essence of *Kim* drained out of it. The film was a spy story, but *Kim* is so infinitely more. It is a drifting among the drifting vagabond life of India, too far down to be coloured by any question of state or politics, so evocative that reading it one catches the very scent of dust and withered marigolds and the smoke of little dung fires where the village worthies gather under the peepul tree in the dusk. It has a great deal of beauty, sheer spiritual beauty, and the deep-seeing time-free mysticism of the East, but it is never for an instant guilty of being solemn. No book which had the shameless Kim for its hero could be solemn.

It has a certain kinship with the *Jungle Books*. Kim is situated just as Mowgli is, a boy belonging to one world, thrown into and accepted by another, and faced in the end by the same choice to be made. Mowgli has to choose between the Jungle and the Village, Kim between going back to the world of action for which he has been trained, and remaining in the completely Eastern world to which he has wandered with his beloved lama; and though we are not specifically told so, we know that he too will go back to the Village, leaving the Jungle behind him, and that he too will break his heart in doing it. Like Mowgli, too, Kim has his sponsors in his adoptive world, four of them; foremost the lama himself, surely the most perfectly good character that Kipling ever created; the lean, ferocious Pathan horse dealer, Mahbub Ali; the smooth soft-bellied Bengali Babu with the heart of a lion, and the masterful old dowager from Saharumpore, whose constant chatter so much bothered the lama.

Kim is I think chiefly for the older child (it was not, when all's said and done, written for children at all), and not every child, even of those who like Kipling, will appreciate it. But those who do will probably get drunk on it, as I did. It is a heady brew, with its constantly changing scenes, its smells and colour and crowding drift of events and people and half-glimpsed glories. But it is the kind of drunkenness which any child would be the richer for afterward.

VII. Primitive Noises

Stalky & Co. failed entirely with me at our first acquaintance, maybe because I was a little too young for it, though I *was* ten, but chiefly I think because my mother read it to me, and of all Kipling's stories it is the only one that does not seem to me to read aloud well. Maybe it is too full of primitive noises, the war chants of,

> 'Ti-hi! Tungalee!
> I eat um pea! I pick um pea!'

with its answering defiance, 'Ingle-go-jang, my joy, my joy!' being notable examples.

A year or so later I read it again, to myself this time, fell instantly under its spell, and must have re-read it with the delight of returning to old friends, and with much unholy laughter, at least a dozen times since then. It was something quite new in school stories, as the *Jungle Books* were something quite new in animal stories; the first of a new kind of book altogether (*Huckleberry Finn* is another of the brotherhood) which combine minute correctness of detail in depicting a way of life, together with a heightening of all its exploits. No ordinary schoolboy could bring off the diabolical exploits which Stalky, Turkey and Beetle carry through to a triumphant conclusion, but they are the kind that every schoolboy dreams of carrying through, like the perfect retort that one thinks of when it is just too late to use it. The book was greeted by a storm of contradictory opinion when it first appeared, for its casual brutalities and its somewhat harsh realism shocked a generation with more evangelical ideas of what a school book should be, and who feared that it would have a demoralising effect on the young. *Tom Brown's Schooldays* has more of really beastly cruelty in it by far than *Stalky* has, but it also has an obvious moral, and the good folk who were shocked by *Stalky*, forgave *Tom Brown* its brutalities for the sake of its moral, and never noticed that *Stalky* has its moral too, though of a subtler kind, and more decently hidden.

Incidentally, I have heard people doubt the wisdom of giving certain books of Kipling's, *Stalky* foremost among them, to children because of his Jingoistic tendencies. The old, old charge of Jingoism that has been levelled at him ever since Britain began to be ashamed of having (or having had) an Empire. The truth is that in all Kipling's works, even in such poems as *The White Man's Burden*, which sometimes sound odd and high-flown in our modern ears, the accent is not on dominion, but on service, and it does a child no harm to get the idea that service is not something to be ashamed of. And if anyone still doubts, let him, oh, do let him, read the chapter of *Stalky*, called *The Flag of their Country*, which concerns the doings of the Jelly-bellied Flag-flapper I have mentioned before, and in which Kipling paints a dazzling portrait of the kind of Jingoist he himself has been accused of being. The gentleman in question, an M.P. of vast unction and many chins, is addressing the school, very much against the school's will, on the subject of patriotism.

'In a raucous voice he cried aloud little matters like the hope of Honour and the dream of Glory, that boys do not discuss even with their most intimate equals; cheerfully assuming that, until he spoke, they had never considered these possibilities. He pointed them to shining goals, with fingers which smudged out all radiance on all horizons. He profaned the most secret places of their souls with outcries and gesticulations. He bade them consider the deeds of their ancestors in such fashion that they were flushed to their tingling ears. Some of them—the rending voice cut a frozen stillness—might have had relatives who perished in the defence of their country. (They thought, not a few of them, of an old sword in a passage, or above a breakfast-room table, seen and fingered by stealth since they could walk.) He adjured them to emulate those illustrious examples; and they looked all ways in their extreme discomfort.'

The reference to the sword and the breakfast-room shows how much of a period piece *Stalky* is now, but if the trappings have changed, the boys and the ideal exploits have not very much, and it remains one of the very few school stories which are also literature, and which I personally would try on any child in search of a boy's school story, whose reading I really cared about.

* * *

The *Just So Stories* are as full of primitive noises as *Stalky*, and yet they, of all Kipling's stories, *must* be read aloud. Read to oneself they are poor things shorn of half their glory. Of what use is an incantation merely thought within one's head and not cried aloud to the stars? The *Just So Stories* are the true stuff of incantation and magic-making, with the inspired repetition of words and phrases ('You must *not* forget the suspenders, Best Beloved,') which is a necessary part of all the best magic and greatly beloved by most small children, though Dr Tompkins quotes one infant as saying in exasperation, 'You needn't say that again.' The first three-quarters of the book can be read to the very smallest children, and they will enjoy the incantation even if they do not always quite grasp what it is all about. This perhaps accounts for the fact that some of the stories have been issued separately in the U.S.A. in picture book form. The last two stories, *The Cat that Walked by Himself* and *The Butterfly that Stamped*, seem to me to be in a different category, possibly because they were written after small Josephine's death. They are more complex, and they go deeper than any of the earlier ones, except the two tales of Taffy and her father. *The Butterfly* is charming and exquisite, a story like a fragment of Eastern filigree work and luminous with a particularly lovely kind of laughter; the story of *The Cat*, seen in a kind of rainy witchlight, has a really back-hair-disturbing magic of its own. (But few children are disturbed by the things that seem to us to have the potency and terror of the true Other World; they keep their fears for the things that no adult would expect them to be afraid of. I know a pillar of the publishing world who admits to having been scared out of his wits by *Alice in Wonderland* when he was seven. *I* had a spiritual horror of pearl buttons. Neither of us felt anything about *The Cat that Walked by Himself*, save that it was a very exciting and very satisfying story and that the cat was superbly catly.)

My own early favourites among the *Just So Stories* were the two tales of Taffy and her father Tegumai, the first largely because it made me laugh until I curled up like an earwig, and the second for the sake of that wonderful alphabet necklace, chronicled bead by bead; but also because of the sense of safety and being beloved which enfolds the naughty small heroine, as though her father had spread a cloak over his Little Girl-Daughter to keep out the cold. I re-read the *Just So Stories* before writing this, and was struck afresh by the depth of feeling not so much in the story but flowing out from it to the child for whom it was told, which makes it almost painfully touching, when one remembers small Josephine. Only twice in all his writings, Kipling cries out for the lost child: once in *They* and once in the song that goes with Taffy, the song beginning, 'There runs a road by Merrow Down', which ends,

> 'In mocassins and deerskin cloak,
> Unfearing, free and fair she flits,
> And lights her little damp-wood smoke
> To show her Daddy where she flits
>
> For far—oh, very far behind,
> So far she cannot call to him,
> Comes Tegumai alone to find
> The daughter that was all to him.'

And to my mind, Taffy's song is the more moving of the two.

Incidentally, like *Peter Rabbit*, the *Just So Stories*, with their camels most 'scruciating idle, and their Parsees with hats from which the rays of the sun were reflected in more-than-Oriental-splendour, are the answer to the people who think that one should not use long words in writing for children. Half the glory of the *Just So Stories*, as I remember across thirty years, was the glory of their long words. I didn't always (I didn't often) understand what they meant, but that was not of the least consequence. They tasted superb.

VIII. The Captains and the Kings

I did not come to *Captains Courageous* until well after I was grown up, and so my approach to it is quite different from my approach to any other of the books gathered here. I can stand back and look at it dispassionately, because I am not emotionally involved. I enjoyed it enormously for a wonderfully detailed account of life in the cod fisheries of the Grand Banks. I was deeply moved by the story of Penn, the 'half-caulked' member of the *We're Here*'s crew, who had been a Moravian pastor, and, seeing his wife and children killed by a flood before his eyes, had lost his identity. When, at another man's need, his memory returned for a space, I felt that I could not bear it; and when, the need being over, the memory and the man's dignity went again, leaving only poor little twittering half-caulked Penn behind, I could bear it less than ever. I suffered one of the coldest cold chills I have ever experienced when the two days dead and sea-buried French sailor returned to claim his brass-mounted knife with which he had killed a man, and I have read few more exciting 'speed pieces' than the account of the multi-millionaire's dash across America in his own private car (it took me some time to realise that it was what we should call a private railway coach) to meet his long-lost son. And yet *Captains Courageous* is the only one among the books dealt with here that I have never wanted to read again.

I was going to complain that there is no shape to the story, but neither is there any shape to speak of to *Kim*, and the moment I open *Kim*, for the third or the eighth or the dozenth time, something in me leaps up in the certainty that I am going to find delight in every page. *Captains Courageous* has no shimmering and crowding riches to compare with *Kim*, and no characters that spring out and lay hold and remain with one afterwards, as the other book has. Of the two boy heroes, Kim, through all his steady development of character, remains most gloriously and consistently and vividly Kim. But Harvey Cheyne, the unpleasant son of the multi-millionaire, having fallen overboard from his ship and been picked up by the *We're Here*, gives one exhibition of frightfulness, and being knocked into the scuppers by the Master, undergoes a change of heart so sudden as to be, to my mind, unconvincing, and becomes thereafter a different person.

Nevertheless, I should rate *Captains Courageous* as a fine story for any boy who likes to read about the sea and sea-faring men. It will carry him along with the swing of the long sea swells from the first page to the last, and when he gets to the last page, any ideas that he has absorbed on the way will be sound ones.

Last of all, *Puck of Pook's Hill* and *Rewards and Fairies*, for like the *Jungle Books*, both *Puck* books must be considered together. In my childhood, I enjoyed *Puck of Pook's Hill* best. I have found that to be the case with most children, and the reason is simple; the stories were written for two real children, Kipling's own John and Elsie, who were the originals of Dan and Una, and they took more than five years to write. The children were only seven and eight when they made their play of Puck and Titania, with the paper donkey's head. They were thirteen and fourteen when *Rewards and Fairies* was published, and the stories had kept pace with them. And therefore, although both series follow on from each other and appear to be for the same age group, those in *Rewards* are actually way above the head of the child who is just able comfortably to manage those in *Puck of Pook's Hill*, not of course that one can really talk of age groups in this particular connection, since Kipling wrote his books on so many levels. As he himself writes of the *Puck* stories,

'I worked the material in three or four overlaid tints and textures, which might or might not reveal themselves according to the shifting light of sex, youth and experience. The tales had to be read by children, before people realised that they were meant for grown-ups.'

The fact remains that most of the children who delight in *Puck of Pook's Hill* will find *Rewards and Fairies* difficult, and have to come to it later.

It is a more highly evolved piece of work than *Puck*; there is in the first book nothing to touch the silver-point delicacy, the quietness as of a country seen in level evening light, of *Marklake Witches* with its haunting accompanying poem *The Way Through the Woods*, nothing that pierces as deep into the very root of things as the pathetic and terrible story of *The Knife and the Naked Chalk*, nothing to touch the rich irony of *The Wrong Thing*. Yet somehow one gets the impression that the first series was written 'as a bird sings' and the second series was not, and the things that one remembers most belong to the first book; Parnesius marching his cohort up to the old gateway into Valentia and finding the arch bricked up and *Finis* scrawled on the dead end; the vivid and most beautiful picture of Sir Richard Dalyngridge crossing the stream on his great white horse. The people of some of the later stories seem less memorable than those of the first book, more perfectly fashioned but less instantly alive. I have even been bored by the American stories. And the *Tree of Justice*, the last story of all, and the most difficult with its strange undertones, which I love and always have loved very greatly, more perhaps than any single story in *Puck of Pook's Hill*, is another tale told by Sir Richard. So perhaps after all, it is just that meeting Sir Richard and Parnesius first, all the later comers are thrown a little into their shadow.

But as Professor Carrington points out, neither Parnesius nor Sir Richard, Dan nor Una, nor even Puck, are the true heroes of the *Puck* books. The true hero is old Hobden, the hedger and past master in the delicate art of poaching, who typifies the tough, earthy life of the countryman, persisting, rooted in his own land, through all the rootless changes that come and go. For the true theme of both books is the Land and the People, the continuity of life; the twentieth-century shepherd linked with the poor puzzled Stone Age hero who bought protection for the sheep, and then found that he must pay not only with the agreed loss of an eye, but with the cold burden of Godhead. Mr Springett the builder's tale of saving the Squire from an unwanted ha ha, which so exactly echoes the story of Sir Harry Dawe's knighthood, across four hundred years. The watermill below the forge that both Parnesius and Sir Richard knew. . . .

And that is one of the greatest values of both books. Children are prone to grow up seeing history as a series of small static pictures, all belonging to Then and having nothing to do with Now. The two *Puck* books, stories and songs alike, with their linking of past and present in one corner of England, must help them to feel it as a living and continuous process of which they themselves are a part, must help them to be at least a little aware of their own living roots behind them, and so see their own times in better perspective than they might otherwise have done.

ix. Kipling Today

It has been a labour of delight to me to put together this short sketch of Kipling as a writer for children, because of all the writers of my childhood, he made the strongest impact on me, an impact which I have never forgotten. There were other books that I loved as much: *The Wind in the Willows*, *Winnie the Pooh*, *Hero Myths and Legends of the British Race*, and a slim, tattered copy of Hans Andersen's *Little Mermaid*, spring to my mind at once; also Lord Lytton's *Last Days of Pompeii*, which now strikes me as the most depressing piece of long-winded Victoriana. But never more than one book or story by any particular author, and never any that have stayed with me more vividly.

Mowgli and Bagheera (but chiefly Bagheera) enriched my make-believe world. *Stalky* and the *Just So Stories* furnished me with things to chant. Parnesius gave me my first feeling for Roman Britain, filling my small opening mind with a splendour as of distant trumpets, long before I had the least idea what the Roman Empire was all about, and when I pictured Maximus's white buckskin leggings laced with gold as being exactly like the knee-high gaiters with buttons all up the sides, in which my own unwilling legs were encased in the winter.

But all that was twenty-five or thirty years ago, and some of the stories were dated even then, though the dating is all on the surface and never in the fundamental things. The question then arises: what is Kipling's place in the world of children's literature today?

Miss Eileen Colwell, until 1967 the Children's Librarian

of the Borough of Hendon, suggests that in this country he lives mainly by virtue of the *Just So Stories* and the *Jungle Books*, both of which are used in library story-hours, often read by teachers to their classes, included in school reading lists, and bestowed on children by parents who loved them in their own childhood. And with the children themselves, from the ages of six to twelve, all three books are very popular. The favourite *Just So* story is undoubtedly *How the Elephant got his Trunk*. As one eight-year-old boy explained, 'The elephant story was the best, because he spanked all his relations.' Of the stories included in the *Jungle Books*, a ten-year-old girl chooses, just as I did myself at her age, *Rikki-Tikki-Tavy* and *The White Seal*; but *Toomai of the Elephants* seems to be the general favourite, though a good proportion of the boys, many of them Wolf Cubs themselves, prefer the Mowgli Stories. *Kim* is only for the out-of-the-ordinary child, and the same applies to *Captains Courageous*; while one eleven-year-old, asked by one of Miss Colwell's branch librarians for his opinion of *Stalky & Co.*, said that his Dad had told him it was a school story, but it wasn't a bit like any other school story he had read.

Puck of Pook's Hill and *Rewards and Fairies* are, sad to say, in almost total eclipse. The schools make no use of them, which seems surprising, and the children say that they dislike short stories, at any rate on historical subjects; and complain that fairies (Puck) are childish. This last reveals a particularly sorry state of affairs, since Puck, despite the canterbury-bell hat, which I have always myself felt to be regrettable, belongs to the true, fairy kind, the ancient aristocracy of the Lordly Ones, the People of the Hills; and such a criticism, levelled at him blindly, shows the damage that has been done by certain children's writers, who by their artless tales of tinsel-and-flower-petal creatures and wee, wee pixies living in wee, wee toadstool houses, have brought his whole race into disrepute, and robbed the modern child of a host of splendours.

There it is; a somewhat disappointing, though challenging picture to a Kipling addict such as myself. But strangely enough, in parts of the world in which one would expect children to be more essentially modern in outlook, and impatient of tradition, more aware of the dating in fact, the picture is a good deal brighter. The Librarian in charge of the Public Library Service to Children in Toronto (where in the children's rooms and school libraries, there are children of every nationality, race and colour), tells me that Kipling is a very favourite subject for library talks, that the *Jungle Books* and *Just So Stories* are constantly used in story-hours, while the books themselves are scarcely ever on the shelves. She also reports some of the children's views, notably one boy on *Captains Courageous*: 'It's a great story! The kid's stuck on himself and he smokes a cigarette and falls overboard and he thinks he can buy off the men on the other boat to take him home. Is he ever spoilt! It's great, you should read it!' A younger one on the *Jungle Books*: 'I like Kipling's books better than any others. I like the way they call it the Red Flower when they mean fire.' And a twelve-year-old with a sister of ten to whom one's heart goes out in sympathy: 'She doesn't like *Stalky*, so I'm reading it to her. I *want* her to like it. I love it.'

Kipling has so much to give to children still, of the things that do not date at all; worthwhile values to set against those of the horror comic; a rich and evocative use of language; stories, never ordinary, in which, because of that gift of his for writing about all things and people from the inside out instead of from the outside in, it is especially easy for the reader or read-to to perform the minor miracle of self-identification which so much helps a small growing mind to stretch itself and open out.

By no means every child will like Kipling, even his *Jungle Books* and *Just So Stories*; and those for whom the penny does not drop and the bell does not ring, will probably dislike him very much indeed, for he is one of those writers about whom there can be no half measures. But every child should have a chance, by having one or other of the books put into his hands at the right moment, to discover for himself whether he likes Kipling or not. Because the child who has never run with Mowgli's wolfpack, or stood with Parnesius and Pertinax to defend the Northern Wall, or thrust a very dead cat under the floor of a rival dormitory to the full length of his arm and Beetle's brolly, has missed something that he will not get from any other writer.

BOOKS BY RUDYARD KIPLING
(WHICH ARE NOW AVAILABLE)
OF INTEREST TO CHILDREN

BOOKS BY RUDYARD KIPLING (WHICH ARE NOW AVAILABLE) OF INTEREST TO CHILDREN

*(All Kipling's prose works are published in this country
by Messrs Macmillan & Co. Ltd)*

Title	Date of first publication	Present available editions
The Jungle Book	1894	Library Edition. Illustrated. Ex. crown 8vo.
		Young People's Edition. Illustrated. Ex. crown 8vo.
		Pocket Edition. Illustrated. F'cap 8vo.
		School Edition. Gl. 8vo.
The Second Jungle Book	1895	Library Edition. Illustrated. Ex. crown 8vo.
		Young People's Edition. Illustrated. Ex. crown 8vo.
		Pocket Edition. Illustrated. F'cap 8vo.
		Overseas Edition. Crown 8vo.
		School Edition. Gl. 8vo.
Captains Courageous	1896-7	Library Edition. Illustrated. Ex. crown 8vo.
		Young People's Edition. Illustrated. Ex. crown 8vo.
		Pocket Edition. Illustrated. F'cap 8vo.
		School Edition. Gl. 8vo.
Stalky & Co.	1899	Library Edition. Illustrated. Ex. crown 8vo.
		Young People's Edition. Illustrated. Ex. crown 8vo.
		Pocket Edition. Illustrated. F'cap 8vo.

Kim	1900-1	Illustrated by Stuart Tresilian. Demy 8vo.
		Library Edition. Illustrated. Ex. crown 8vo.
		Young People's Edition. Illustrated. Ex. crown 8vo.
		Pocket Edition. Illustrated. F'cap 8vo.
		School Edition. Gl. 8vo.
Just So Stories	1902	Illustrated by the author. 4to.
		Library Edition. Illustrated. Ex. crown 8vo.
		Young People's Edition. Illustrated. F'cap 8vo.
		Pocket Edition. Illustrated. F'cap 8vo.
		School Edition. Gl. 8vo.
Puck of Pook's Hill	1906	Library Edition. Illustrated. Ex. crown 8vo.
		Young People's Edition. Illustrated. Ex. crown 8vo.
		Pocket Edition. Illustrated. F'cap 8vo.
		Overseas Edition. Crown 8vo.
		School Edition. Gl. 8vo.
Rewards and Fairies	1910	Library Edition. Illustrated. Ex. crown 8vo.
		Young People's Edition. Illustrated. Ex. crown 8vo.
		Pocket Edition. Illustrated. F'cap 8vo.
Animal Stories (compiled as follows:)	1932	Illustrated by Stuart Tresilian. Crown 4to.

The Camel's Hump (poem) from *Just So Stories*
The Cat that Walked by Himself from *Just So Stories*
Pussy Can Sit by the Fire and Sing (poem) from *Just So Stories*
The Conversion of St Wilfrid from *Rewards and Fairies*
Garm, a Hostage from *Actions and Reactions*

The White Seal from *The Jungle Book*
The Maltese Cat from *The Day's Work*
Lukannon (poem) from *The Jungle Book*
How Fear Came from *The Second Jungle Book*
The Law of the Jungle (poem) from *The Second Jungle Book*
My Lord the Elephant from *Many Inventions*
I Keep Six Honest Serving Men (poem) from *Just So Stories*
Rikki-Tikki-Tavy from *The Jungle Book*
Darzee's Chaunt (poem) from *The Jungle Book*
Moti Guj—Mutineer from *Life's Handicap*
I Will Remember What I Was (poem) from *The Jungle Book*
Private Learoyd's Story from *Soldiers Three*
Toomai of the Elephants from *The Jungle Book*
Parade Song of the Camp Animals (poem) from *The Jungle Book*

All the Mowgli Stories (compiled from *The Jungle Book* and *The Second Jungle Book*)	1933	Illustrated by Stuart Tresilian. Crown 4to.
The Maltese Cat	1955	Illustrated by Lionel Edwards. Pott. 4to.

Walter de la Mare

LEONARD CLARK

CONTENTS

H

1. Introductory

'Children . . . live in a world peculiarly
their own, so much so that it is doubtful if the adult can do more than very
fleetingly reoccupy that far away
consciousness.'

Walter de la Mare. *Rupert
Brooke and the Intellectual
Imagination.* (1919)

So wrote Walter de la Mare—with doubts as to how far
adults can write even fairly successfully *about* children, let
alone completely understand them.

When the first illustrated edition of *Peacock Pie* appeared
in December 1916 with Heath Robinson's amusing and
delightful drawings, the *Times Literary Supplement* hailed
the poems as '. . . the purest poetry for children ever made;
Blake and Stevenson not forgotten'. Later on, in 1932, in
his essay, *Lewis Carroll*, Walter de la Mare was to say,

'Yet writers who had the nursery in view, and even long
after William Blake had sung of innocence, remain for the
most part convinced that what is good for the young *must*
be unpleasant. Their rhymes like their prose were "nearly
always in a moral, minor or miserable key". They prescribed
not simples, syrups and cordials, but brimstone . . . A
reaction, it is clear, was bound to follow, and that reaction
has perhaps reached its extreme in a good deal of the
nursery literature of our own day, which is as silly, if not
worse, as theirs was dismal.'

Walter de la Mare—and the work of W. B. Yeats has been borne in mind—is the greatest writer of English lyrical poetry (particularly for children) of the first half of this century. It is tendentious and futile to label this poetry as being merely 'minor' or 'Georgian' or 'romantic'. And it is patronising and insulting to say of this poetry that it is little more than 'accomplished'. Yet this is what some critics, who have lost their sense of wonder, have said of it because it does not measure up to what *they* say poetry ought to be.

For the facts are (as will be proved, it is hoped, later on in this monograph) that Walter de la Mare was a consistent and resolute writer, a master of the English language both in prose and poetry, and one who has delighted—and will continue to delight—generations of readers of diverse gifts, beliefs and social class. He possessed an unusual talent—an individual vision, and this talent is unsurpassed in power and significance by any English poet within the field he made peculiarly his own. His poetry had no period limitations. Time, which did not over-praise him in his own day, will not belittle him when it comes to the final reckoning.

His work is always found on the shelves of children's libraries, and librarians continue to recommend successive generations of children to read it. His poetry and his stories for children are firmly established in the schools of this country, of the Commonwealth, and of America. Eleanor Farjeon wrote of her visits with Walter de la Mare to,

'. . . Girls' Schools and Children's Libraries, he to read his poems and I to sing my nursery rhymes, for I was always shy of reading aloud in public, or indeed of appearing on any platform for any reason. Oddly enough, I felt he liked support almost as much as I needed it, and even asked me to split his occasions with him. Children adored his presence among them, but I sometimes wondered if his small rapt listeners heard him beyond the third row, for he read his poems to them in the same reflective voice with which, in the intimacy of his room, poetry fell with ease into the talk. He would tell them, "This one is called 'The Little Green Orchard'... and here's another one... and another... and here's another ..." Once, when I had written describing a prize-giving I had braced myself to attend alone, he wished he had been there "disguised as a little creature with blue ribbons in her hair and a muslin frock"; and in turn described one of his own recent prize-givings at a girls' school—"and it was awful to feel the smile from the heart steadily stiffening into the plaster of Paris of habit—and *yet* to be coming from the same place, I believe".'

James Southall Wilson, former Edgar Allan Poe Professor of Literature at the University of Virginia, wrote of Walter de la Mare, in the National Book League's de la Mare number of *Books* in May 1956, that in the 1920's,

'He was a new voice, fresh, individual, and authentic. His public was not so large, but it was almost passionately devoted to his work. During the period when poetic romance was current, de la Mare enjoyed his greatest popularity along with W. H. Hudson, Arthur Machen, James Stephens, and Algernon Blackwood. But in America it was as a poet rather than as a prose writer that de la Mare was best known. Even today more people associate him with his verse for children, especially his *Peacock Pie*, than with any other phase of his work.... de la Mare's poetry is still well known in the States. He is also familiar as an anthologist, especially through his volume, *Come Hither*. His American publisher reports that the following titles are still in print: *Memoirs of a Midget*, *Broomsticks*, *Selected Tales of Walter de la Mare*, *The Three Royal Monkeys*, *Told Again*, *Behold This Dreamer*, and *Come Hither*. All these books have a steady sale though none is in great demand. As a writer of prose he was more widely read in America thirty or even twenty years ago than now. . . . When taste in America swings back (as of course it will), for a time at least, to beauty and form in literature, de la Mare will be more recognized for his exquisite and rare art, not only as a novelist and poet but especially in his unique short stories.'

And Eileen Colwell, an expert in the field of children's books, when asked, in 1957, by the editor of *The Horn Book Magazine* (a de la Mare memorial number) 'What is your favourite de la Mare book?' replied,

'Of all poets and storytellers, Walter de la Mare has given me the deepest joy. After the strange and profound fantasy of *The Three Royal Monkeys*, two short stories are my favourites, perhaps because I have shared them so often with children.

'The first is the lovely tale of *The Three Sleeping Boys of Warwickshire*, three little chimney sweeps whose sooty bodies are separated from their dream-shapes by the greed of old Nollykins. For fifty-three years the boys sleep on until one April morning they are awakened by a girl's kiss on their "stone-cold mouths" and, their dream-shapes home at last, they leap out into the glory of Spring. So wonderfully is the ecstasy of Spring and its new life conveyed that I can never finish the story without a lift of the heart.

'My second choice is *The Old Lion*, the story of the friendship between the sailor, Mr Bumps, and Jasper, the little monkey he buys in "a village of black men". So perceptive is Walter de la Mare's understanding of Jasper's loneliness and dignity in his alien captivity that as we watch Jasper we too feel a "peculiar coldness" stealing through our blood. When Mr Bumps has to leave Jasper on the African shore, a stranger to his own people also, we feel as grieved as the sailor himself. A haunting and moving story.

'These two stories contain for me the very essence of Walter de la Mare's genius, beauty, wisdom, passionate concern for all unhappiness, and his consummate literary skill.'

Walter de la Mare wrote steadily for sixty years, seeking to perfect his craftsmanship and to develop that rare talent to the full; he succeeded in doing so in a score or so of poems and in a dozen or so of tales. These wear the bloom of immortality. How many writers ever do as much, for all the books they write? His imagination was unique, particularly in his own day, though of the same cast as Coleridge's and Poe's; he was blessed with foreknowledge and an uncanny understanding of children and their world; he knew by heart as well as by intellect what are the salient characteristics of childhood. Neither was he led astray by the more paradisal aspects of childhood, by the 'trailing clouds of glory'. He saw it, as D. H. Lawrence did, and Wordsworth did not, as a whole thing, divine, elemental, wayward, unfathomable. His learning, which he wore modestly with gossamer lightness, was wide and selective. He shared with Edmund Blunden and E. H. Meyerstein (who were two of his friends) the distinction of having explored more of the byways of reading than most other writers of his time. If there was an English classic (particularly a Victorian one which had been temporarily forgotten) he had not read, this did not reveal itself to those who knew him with any intimacy. As an editor, and collector of folk tales, of traditional stories and poems, he had few peers. His introduction, for instance, to *Animal Stories*, is a brilliant dissertation on folk-lore. He wrote three very original novels for adults, *Henry Brocken*, *The Return*, and *Memoirs of a Midget*. *The Return* and *Memoirs of a Midget* were awarded literary prizes and both have been translated into several other languages. He wrote *The Three Mulla-Mulgars*, one of the finest long stories for children ever written—a book of poetic truth and beauty, tender, fresh, and shimmering with the light of its faraway snows. There are also a fairy play, *Crossings* (written for a boys' school), some fifty short stories (including twenty or so for children), re-writings of traditional and Bible tales for children, any number of critical essays ranging over a wide field and displaying unusual insight and knowledge, anthologies of poems for children in schools, four massive and masterly anthologies for grown ups: *Desert Islands*, *Early One Morning in the Spring*, *Behold, This Dreamer*, *Love*, and one, *Come Hither*, of poetry only, 'for the young of all ages': these are concerned with the world of poetry, exploration, childhood, dreams and love. They would have made a reputation in themselves. And it is unlikely that they will not be read and used as sources of reference for years to come.

His extraordinary imagination is further illustrated by *A Child's Day* and *Flora*. In *A Child's Day* he wrote rhymes to illustrate a set of fine photographs of a child, portraying her at work and play from dawn to dusk. And in *Flora* he composed poems to accompany the aquarelle drawings of Pamela Bianco, a child herself, barely in her 'teens. It is staggering to realise that there are nearly a hundred and fifty first and variant editions of books by Walter de la Mare, all published between 1902 and 1956. And yet he did not become an established writer until he was over forty years old. And if this output were not enough, he made over sixty contributions to books by other writers, including fifty introductions, prefaces and forewords.

Walter de la Mare was the complete professional writer with the professional's attitude to his work. He slogged at words all his life, as hard as any navvy with pick and shovel.

WALTER DE LA MARE

Writing *was* his life. Apart from a solitary visit to America
in 1916, he never left the shores of England. His life was
almost without incident. He married, had four children, and
eleven grandchildren. He was honoured by his country
(Order of Merit; Companion of Honour) and by five British
universities. Yet he himself would have said that his life was
always interesting and exciting, though he preferred its
pattern to be quiet and unsensational. He saw many changes
of fashion for he lived in six reigns. Born in an old queen's,
and dying in a young queen's, reign, he knew the horrors of
three major wars, each worse than the one before. And
eventually 'Walter de la Mare' became a household name
because of the children who were introduced to his poems
and stories in schools and libraries.

II. The Man

Walter John de la Mare was born at Charlton, a village then, in the county of Kent, on 25th April, 1873. Dickens, one of his heroes, had only been dead for three years; Wilkie Collins, another, was still alive. Tennyson, the Poet Laureate, and Browning were at the height of their fame; Hardy's *Under the Greenwood Tree* was about to be issued. It is not often realised how much of a Victorian de la Mare was, and remained, at heart (he is included in the *Oxford Book of Victorian Verse*), nor who were his contemporaries and earliest influences.

His father, James Edward de la Mare, descended from an old Huguenot family, was a Civil Servant. As he was born in 1811 he was sixty-two when his famous son was born. He died when the boy was four years old. So Walter de la Mare was brought up by his mother, Lucy Sophia, the daughter of a naval surgeon, Dr Colin Browning, of Scottish descent. The mother had a great influence on him and he was devoted to her. Lucy was his favourite Christian name and it appears over and over again in his poems and stories. Certainly the early years made a deep impression upon his heart and mind. From his mother he heard many of the nursery rhymes, legends, fairy tales and traditional poems which were to be his life-long delight, and which, in due course, he was to add to and enrich.

When the father died, the family moved from Charlton to London and Walter de la Mare became a chorister of St Paul's Cathedral, receiving his education at its famous choir school, then in Carter Lane. He was a good student and before he left had made a name for himself as the founder and editor of *The Choristers' Journal* (his first venture into editorship), which appeared in cyclostyle in 1889 and 1890. He left school, and the choir (after singing at the old Queen's Golden Jubilee service in St Paul's) at the age of fourteen, to become a clerk in the City offices of the Anglo-American Oil Company, in whose service he was to remain for nearly twenty years. But in his spare time— such as it was—he was writing short stories and poems, and, what is more, getting some of the stories published in *The Cornhill*, *Pall Mall Gazette*, *Black and White* and *The Sketch*. Yet he was so shy about it all that he wrote under the pseudonym of 'Walter Ramal', the 'Ramal' being a play on his surname. His first book of poems, *Songs of Childhood*, appeared in 1902. It was well received by the critics but few copies were sold. However, a new poet of childhood had obviously arrived on the scene. His first novel, *Henry Brocken*, came in 1904, and *Poems*, two years later. And in 1908, with few prospects, but with high hopes and a belief that he could live by writing what *he* wanted to write, he left the oil company for good and became a full-time author. His second novel, *The Return*, appeared in 1910 and brought him rather more into the public gaze. And, in the same year, *The Three Mulla-Mulgars*, the delicious story of Thumb, Thimble and Nod, the adventuring royal monkeys, was published; this book is now called *The Three Royal Monkeys*. But it was Walter de la Mare's book of rhymes, with the inviting title of *Peacock Pie*, published in 1913, which was to establish him as 'the true inheritor of the nursery rhyme', which is what Victoria Sackville-West called him. From that day he never looked back; until he died in 1956, loved and honoured the world over, childhood was one of his major themes. To the end of his days he strove to bring home to his readers its characteristics of innocence, delight, imagination and deep feeling. And he made no distinction of quality whether he wrote for adults or children.

To meet this man was an unforgettable experience, as hundreds of his friends and chance acquaintances can testify. The great man and the great writer were, in him, inseparable, which is not always the case. He was about five feet eight inches tall, with a head that could have served for the statue of a Roman emperor, so commanding and clearcut was its modelling. The ears were large, pricked, so it sometimes seemed, to the listening of things which others could not hear. The lips were firm and gentle; the voice soft, but wonderfully resonant, made the most of cadences, and had the faintest hint of an accent which betrayed the Londoner. The face had nothing mean or gross about it, but was alive with meaning and purpose. Walter de la Mare, in his poem *The Visionary*, could have been describing his own face.

> 'A face like amber, pale and still
> With eyes of light, unchangeable,
> Whose grave and steadfast scrutiny
> Pierced through all earthly memory.'

But it was the dark eyes which attracted so powerfully. They have often been described as birdlike. But of what bird? The eagle or the robin? They were certainly intense. They missed nothing. They observed all the signs of the changing and returning seasons. A dropped feather, a staring berry, a flake of snow, a clockless snail—these eyes *saw*, and memory and divining imagination retained for ever. They asked questions and often gave the answers to the questions without a word being said. They were eyes that welcomed and rarely knew the darknesses of pique or anger. They pinpointed but enfolded at the same time.

The hands, too, rarely moved to emphasise, and the smile only occasionally developed into laughter out loud. But it convulsed itself by a lowering of the eyelids and a puckering up of every facial muscle. And once the floodgates of speech were opened, what wisdom would then be let loose—a waterfall of English words, beautifully spoken.

There can hardly ever have been a kinder or gentler man. He honoured the whole of creation, children and animals most of all. He had always something good to say, even about the smart modern critics of his work, something encouraging, something which summed up the situation generously and compassionately. Silence, yes, if books and things and people were not appreciated or fully understood, but never anything spiteful or rancorous. Walter de la Mare hated the cold spirit and the pomposity of those who always thought they were right. He was unusually kind to young writers, was always willing to write introductions, and had a generous attitude towards the book he was asked to help, whether it was a story for children, a collection of nursery rhymes, or a list of books for children. He put himself into everything he did, even when he was old and frail.

And how he loved England. He wrote many poems about his native land and always regretted that he did not fight for her in her wars as so many of his fellow-poets had done. One of his very last poems was called *England*. A mere four lines, it said so much.

> 'All that is dearest to me thou didst give—
> Loved faces, ways, stars, waters, language, sea;
> Through two dark crises in thy Fate I have lived,
>   But—never fought for thee.'

It could truly be said of Walter de la Mare, like the man in Thomas Hardy's poem (and he was a great admirer of Hardy and was influenced by his work), that he was 'A very dear dark-eyed gentleman'. He could never resist requests from children, whether known or unknown to him. He answered their letters, read their poems, and sent them inscribed copies of his books. He gave them hours of precious writing time, and when it was once suggested that he should not write so many letters, he said that he could not turn an angel from his door. Children visited him, came under his spell, and never forgot him.

Pamela Bianco, for whose drawings Walter de la Mare wrote the verses of *Flora*, has told, in *The Horn Book Magazine*, the de la Mare memorial number for June 1957, of her meeting with him.

'In November 1919 my parents, my brother Cecco, and I were going to England to live and I looked forward eagerly to meeting Walter de la Mare. Before leaving Italy I received a letter from the poet, written on grey paper in a delicately lovely and somewhat hieroglyphic handwriting. I treasured that letter and I have kept it so very carefully during these long past years that it still looks as if it had been written only a few days ago.

'We arrived in London on a November evening, and the next morning my father went to Anerley to pay his respects to Walter de la Mare. He was accompanied by Cecco. They returned with a tea and supper invitation from the poet and his wife, for the following Sunday . . . When we stepped out of the station in Anerley, snow was beginning to fall. I remember that we walked along brick pavements and that many of the gardens we passed had hedges with little bright red berries. Presently we came to 14 Thornsett Road, the house in which Walter de la Mare lived. At our knock the front door opened immediately; and there to welcome us, in the gathering dusk, were the poet and his wife, their son, Dick, and their beautiful dark-eyed daughter, Florence.

Although Dick and Florence were only a few years older than I, they both seemed grown up to me. Mrs de la Mare was a lovely person, of very great charm and warmth.

'After removing our wraps, we went into the drawing room where a cheerful log fire was blazing. Still feeling shy, I sat upon a cushion at one side of the fireplace and gazed upward at Walter de la Mare. He looked exactly as I thought a poet should, and both in appearance and in manner lived entirely up to my dreams. He was dressed that day in a navy blue suit; his eyes and hair were dark brown, he had a beautiful classic face which bore an expression of great nobility, and his approach was gentle and warm hearted.'

A nine-year-old boy bullied his long-suffering mother into buying a second-hand copy of *Peacock Pie* for him from a stall in Gloucester market. The boy was greatly taken with *Silver* but thought the poem had blemishes. So he wrote a letter to 'the man with the funny name' c/o G.P.O., objecting to 'shoon' (rhyming with 'moon') as the plural of 'shoes'. Most people wouldn't have bothered to answer. But not Walter de la Mare. He wrote a letter, in his own defence, justifying the grammar and referring the country lad to Chaucer and Webster's Dictionary.

A young girl in a drab town in the Midlands, the child of working-class parents, came across some of his poems for the first time in one of her school books. The experience completely changed her life. She began to keep a diary in which she wrote her thoughts and feelings about the poems. She borrowed more books of de la Mare's poems from her local library. She knew nothing about Walter de la Mare or whether he was alive or dead. She only knew that the poems said something very special to her; she couldn't get *these* poems out of her mind. Her teacher wrote to Walter de la Mare and told him the story, but he was so humbled that he could hardly bring himself to write to the child. However, he did so and thanked her. She was so shy and overcome that she could not send a reply. Eventually the story leaked out and formed the subject of a very sensitive broadcast.

Walter de la Mare died at the age of 83—a child of mature years—and is buried in the crypt of St Paul's Cathedral. His unity with children was as the touch of dew-drop is to rosebud. He was, in fact, a practical mystic, who discovered very early in his life that it was the ugliness of the world which was always threatening to destroy his 'intimations of immortality'. Walter de la Mare was a true and unswerving man who accepted life and came to terms with it. In his closing years he described himself in his poem, *A Portrait*, as:

'Old: yet unchanged;—still pottering in his thoughts;
Still eagerly enslaved by books and print;
Less plagued, perhaps, by rigid musts and oughts,
But no less frantic in vain argument;

Still happy as a child, with its small toys,
Over his inkpot and his bits and pieces,—
Life's arduous, fragile and ingenuous joys,
Whose charm failed never—nay, it even increases'!

and:

'Not yet inert, but with a tortured breast
At hint of that bleak gulf—his last farewell;
Pining for peace, assurance, pause and rest,
Yet slave to what he loves past words to tell;

A foolish, fond old man, his bed-time nigh,
Who still at western window stays to win
A transient respite from the latening sky,
And scarce can bear it when the Sun goes in.'

Until the day of his death he remained a bubbling spring of charmed English water. Many have drunk of that spring, deeply or in sips, but few have done so and not been affected in some measure by its power and enchantment.

III. The Writer

It is now proper to examine in greater detail the claim which has been made for Walter de la Mare that he is a major poet and storyteller for children. But before that is possible, the books he wrote for, and about, children should be listed, though it is not easy to isolate these from the whole corpus of his work. Certainly in many of his books of poetry intended for adults there are poems which are of the very stuff of childhood. With this proviso, then, there are:

POEMS

> *Songs of Childhood.* 1902.
> *A Child's Day.* 1912.
> *Peacock Pie.* 1913. (There are several illustrated editions by W. Heath Robinson, C. Lovat Fraser, Emett and Edward Ardizzone)
> *Down-Adown-Derry.* 1922. (Illustrated by Dorothy Lathrop)
> *Poems for Children.* 1930.
> *This Year, Next Year.* 1937. (With illustrations by Harold Jones)
> *Bells and Grass.* 1941. (With illustrations by Emett)

Poems for Children consisted of selections from earlier books, with twenty new poems. *Collected Rhymes and Verses*, a collection from all previously published books of rhymes, appeared in 1944. Of the books of poems listed, *Songs of Childhood, Peacock Pie, Bells and Grass* and *Collected Rhymes and Verses*, are still in print.

PLAY

Crossings. 1921. (Music by C. Armstrong Gibbs, and decorations by Randolph Schwabe)

STORIES

The Three Mulla-Mulgars. 1910. (Called *The Three Royal Monkeys* since 1935)
Story and Rhyme. 1921.
Miss Jemima. 1925.
Broomsticks and Other Tales. 1925. (With designs by Bold)
Lucy. 1927.
Old Joe. 1927.
Told Again. 1927. (Called *Tales Told Again* since 1959)
Stories from the Bible. 1929.
The Lord Fish and Other Tales. 1933. (Illustrated by Rex Whistler)
Animal Stories. 1939.
Mr Bumps and His Monkey. 1942. (Illustrated by Dorothy Lathrop)
The Old Lion and Other Stories. 1942.
The Magic Jacket and Other Stories. 1944.
The Scarecrow and Other Stories. 1945.
The Dutch Cheese and Other Stories. 1946.

Of these, all are original stories, with the exception of *Told Again*, *Stories from The Bible*, *Animal Stories*, (and, reprinted separately, *Jack and The Beanstalk*, *Dick Whittington* (1951), *Snow White* and *Cinderella* (1952), taken from *Told Again*). In 1947, seventeen of his original stories were published as *Collected Stories for Children*. This collection, *The Three Royal Monkeys* (illustrated by Mildred E. Eldridge), *The Scarecrow and Other Stories*, *Stories from The Bible* and *Animal Stories* are still in print; that is, the bulk of his own, and all the re-told tales.

POETRY ANTHOLOGIES

    Come Hither. 1923. (Embellished by Alec Buckels)
    Tom Tiddler's Ground. 1931. (Selections from other
       poets, illustrated by Bewick woodcuts, and intended
       for schools)
    Old Rhymes and New. 1932. (Selections from his own
       verse, intended for schools)

Of these, by far the most important is *Come Hither*. Both
this and *Tom Tiddler's Ground* are still in print, but not,
alas, the other anthology.

If these lists are studied carefully there emerges a fascinating pattern. Most of the poems and rhymes were written
first (1902-1927) and the stories, apart from *The Three
Mulla-Mulgars*, came next (1925-1942). De la Mare was
primarily a poet.

BOOKS ABOUT CHILDREN AND CHILDHOOD

These were intended for adults and are important contributions to child study and psychology. Of them, the most
important is *Early One Morning in the Spring* (1935), an
educational document of great erudition, a handbook, in
fact, on teaching. There are valuable comments about
children, too, in *Rupert Brooke and the Intellectual Imagination* (1919), (which later appeared as an essay in *Pleasures
and Speculations* (1940)), the story of *Henry Brocken* (1904),
and his 'travels and adventures in the rich, strange, scarce-
imaginable region of romance', and the poignant growing-up
and tragedy of Miss M. in *Memoirs of a Midget* (1921).

Finally, there are the introductions which Walter de la
Mare wrote to other writers' books which deal with various
aspects of childhood. The most important of these are the
introductions to *The Small Years* by Frank Kendon (1930),

Sun Before Seven by Ian Dall (1936), *Nursery Rhymes for Certain Times* (1946, based on a selection made by Roger Ingpen, edited and augmented posthumously by his wife and Miss Mary Grenside) and *When I was a Child* (1946). Unfortunately all these are out of print, but are available from libraries. *When I was a Child* is an anthology edited by Edward Wagenknecht, published in America.

IV. The Poet

In 1943, Richard Church in his *A Twentieth-Century Gallery*, said of de la Mare's poems for children:

'The effect is aeolian. Overtones come sighingly out of his strange, metrical essays. It is like listening to the air, in heavy, frosty weather, humming through the wires near a telegraph pole. A child thinks it is the voice of the messages. A grown-up hears it with a sad nostalgia as the music of time, of vanished humanity, and dreams that are only dreams. The voice passes on, touching the small things of earth, and making them vocal.'

And a quarter of a century before that, the critic of the *Times Literary Supplement* had written in a long essay, *Children and Poetry*:

'Mr de la Mare's verse puts a spell upon them (i.e. children), partly by its music and partly by its rich and quaint fancy. Of these qualities it is probable that the music is the more important. There never was a greater master of delicate and cunning rhythms than Mr de la Mare: and they carry an exquisite vowel melody that haunts the ear of a child who does not even know the meaning of half the words used.'

The secrets of Walter de la Mare's craftsmanship are quaint fancy, vowel melody, and cunning rhythm, all combining to give haunting overtones, strangeness and spellbinding dreams. The strongest influences upon his poetry were Shakespeare (most of de la Mare's fairies come from Shakespeare's England), Christina Rossetti and, to a lesser degree, Robert Louis Stevenson. But it must always be remembered how steeped he was in the knowledge and the spirit of traditional poetry, nursery rhymes, and the Bible.

In *Songs of Childhood*, for instance, Walter de la Mare writes about children, fairies, moonlight, witches, ogres, dwarfs, sleep, England, the miniature, dreamland. The children are called Jane (or Jenny, or Jinny), Timothy, Elaine, Lucy, Ann (or Annie), Mary, John, Susan, Tom. They are very English and late-Victorian children and the fairies come out at nightfall when the moon is shining to look at them. These fairies live 'where the bluebells and the wind are' and 'where the primrose and the dew are', they dance in the early morning or under green willows, and the Prince of Sleep walks with them at evening. The witches are bushes in 'bright scarlet bud' or 'three crows upon a bough', one dwarf lives in Barberry Wood and three others on the Isle of Lone. An ogre prowls on Trebarwith sands. The whole world is full of echoes, secrets and whisperings, footfalls have no sounds and voices begin suddenly, come from nowhere, and then go back into the silences. No strange being is ever seen, but only heard, or felt to be near at hand. It is as if one was brushed across the face by a hand of fur in the darkness. Babies are rocked to sleep, the lamp-lighter goes his rounds, Jane likes 'A bumpity ride in a waggon of hay', John Mouldy sits alone and smiling in his cellar, 'deep down twenty steps of stone', there are rainbows, sunsets, pilgrims, pedlars, fiddlers, millers, a raven's tomb, a christening and a funeral. De la Mare's miniature world is there with the dwarfs and the tiny fly. A sailor 'with painted eyes' surprisingly turns up in an English wood though the geography of it all is Tartary or Urdon or Arrroar or Alulvan. The real rulers of these lands are not the English children, but moonlit dwarfs who are called Alliolyle, Lallerie and Muziomone, whose 'beds they were made of the holly-wood'. The songs of childhood are delicate expressions of a faraway dreamland, set between dawn and

dusk, where the cricket calls. They are sometimes sad and
pining and sometimes not very far from the sinister. The
collection contains at least six poems—*Tartary*, *Bunches of
Grapes*, *John Mouldy*, *The Fly*, *Haunted* and *I Met at Eve*—
which are often found in anthologies. Of these, *Tartary* is a
very familiar de la Mare poem.

> 'If I were Lord of Tartary,
>   Myself and me alone,
> My bed should be of ivory,
>   Of beaten gold my throne;
> And in my court would peacocks flaunt,
> And in my forests tigers haunt,
> And in my pools great fishes slant
>   Their fins athwart the sun.
>
> If I were Lord of Tartary,
>   Trumpeters every day
> To every meal would summon me,
>   And in my courtyard bray;
> And in the evening lamps should shine,
> Yellow as honey, red as wine,
> While harp, and flute, and mandoline,
>   Made music sweet and gay.'

The child in *A Child's Day* is called Elizabeth Ann.
She wakes, gets out of bed, washes, dresses, has her break-
fast, takes her teddy bear for a walk, paddles in a pool,
makes a daisy chain, plays ball, and then has her dinner. This
over, she steals some ginger from the pantry, looks at her
picture books of nursery rhymes and fairy stories, dresses up,
and then has her tea. There follows some cutting out and
some musing before the fire before she goes off to bed.
Elizabeth Ann is a rich child with a well-planned day.
There is much for her to do and enjoy; she has books, toys,
games, pictures and flowers. But she is lonely and there is

no other child for her to play with. We are not even made
aware of her parents, but only of Susan, her nurse, and the
cook. Yet her imagination can wander where it will. *A
Child's Day* is a collection of poems about how a child lives
through a typical day. The verses show how acute de la
Mare's observation of children was (certainly of one child),
and how instinctively he recognised what was best and most
appropriate for her. No other book exists quite like it. It is
a good example, too, of de la Mare's gifts as a rhymester.
And once again we come across the invented names,
Uanjinee, Baddeley, Shieveley, and a fairy singing in a
cherry tree, and there are the pictures which Elizabeth Ann
sees in the fire.

> 'Golden palaces there she sees,
> With fiery fountains, flaming trees;
> Through darkling arch and smouldering glen
> March hosts of little shimmering men,
> To where beneath the burning skies
> A blazing salamander lies,
> Breathing out sparks and smoke the while
> He watches them with hungry smile.'

A Child's Day ends on a sigh.

> 'O then, mourn Baddeley;
> O then, toll Shieveley;
> This brief day now over;
> Life's but a span;
> Tell how my heart aches,
> Tell how my heart breaks,
> To bid now farewell
> To Elizabeth Ann.'

But it is *Peacock Pie* which is de la Mare's masterpiece and
finest memorial as far as his poetry for children is concerned.

And what a title! In its day it was a very popular book of
rhymes and went into innumerable editions. It now exists in
a fine edition illustrated by Edward Ardizzone. *Peacock Pie*
is an extension of the childhood world of the previous books.
It is a world which, full of fantasy and fun, is yet drenched
in moonlight—romantic, brooding, questioning. Ghostly
horsemen ride over the hill, and not so ghostly ones up to
bed, 'someone' knocks at a small door, 'Whatever Miss T.
eats, Turns into Miss T.', there is a cupboard of lollypops
and Banbury cakes, and the boys and girls who dance, or
float, through these pages are called Tim, Ann, Jemima,
Bess, Henry, Jack, Dick and Lucy. These de la Mare children keep dogs and chickens, hate butchers, enjoy stories
of the ship of Rio with a crew of ninety-nine monkeys, of
the Watch trudging to and fro all through the night, of the
old woman who went blackberry picking and met a fairy, of
the thief who came to Robin's castle, of old farmer Turvey
who danced farmers Bates and Giles off the ground. These
children sing, as in *The Quartette*,

> 'Tom sang for joy and Ned sang for joy and old Sam
> sang for joy;
> All we four boys piped up loud, just like one boy;
> And the ladies that sate with the Squire—their cheeks
> were all wet,
> For the noise of the voice of us boys, when we sang
> our Quartette.
>
> Tom he piped low and Ned he piped low and old Sam
> he piped low;
> Into a sorrowful fall did our music flow;
> And the ladies that sate with the Squire vowed they'd
> never forget,
> How the eyes of them cried for delight, when we sang
> our Quartette.'

Peacock Pie also contains widows, sweeps, lonely spinsters, soldiers, sailors, old houses, and a new range of animals, including lion, bear, mole, donkey, pig, cat, and rat—all playing their part in a kind of enchanted children's zoo. Of course, there are witches and fairies with a few change-lings into the bargain, and odd names such as Gimmul, Mel, Melmillo. The terrain seems to be an offshoot of a delightfully mad and inconsequential England, with English trees, and the English seasons, lit always by a wandering full moon, washed by great seas, and humming with sighing winds. Not all children will be able to enter this peacock territory, though many, the more imaginative ones, will do so easily and willingly. For all the changes in the social climate since de la Mare baked his extraordinary pie, the ingredients for children remain the same. Some of the wit and humour will not be obvious to a few, but how many will be able to resist the stories, the beasts, the strange grown-ups, the other children, and the 'othere worlde'? There cannot be many books of poetry with so many poems which have stood up so well to the test of time—*Some One, The Ship of Rio, Miss T., The Cupboard, The Window, Full Moon, The Quartette, Off The Ground, Nicholas Nye, Five Eyes, Silver, The Song of the Mad Prince*—to make but one selection. Children's debt to de la Mare is great because he showed them, as no one had ever shown them before in quite the same way, how to see beauty and wonder in the most unlikely places. For instance, in *Old Shellover*,

> ' "Come!" said Old Shellover.
> "What?" says Creep.
> The horny old Gardener's fast asleep;
> The fat cock Thrush
> To his nest has gone,
> And the dew shines bright

In the rising Moon;
Old Sallie Worm from her hole doth peep;
"Come!" said Old Shellover.
"Ay!" said Creep.'

It is a wonder which remains wonderful because its patina
has the property of being able to stay bright for ever. Shakespeare's fairies in *A Midsummer Night's Dream* and the
spirits from *The Tempest* would quickly recognise themselves in *Peacock Pie*.

In *Down-Adown-Derry*—again a catching title—(it is
the name of a poem in *Songs of Childhood*), de la Mare
brought between two covers all his fairy poems. They are
not all whimsical fairies. There are good and bad ones.
Down-Adown-Derry has its witches, too, and its whispering
verges of dreamland. Many of the poems had previously
appeared in *Songs of Childhood*, *Poems* (1906), *A Child's
Day*, *Peacock Pie*, *The Listeners* (1912), *Motley* (1918),
Poems 1901-1918 (1920), with one poem from *The Three
Mulla-Mulgars*. But there were also about a dozen new
poems, including *Sunk Lyonesse* where,

'The Nereids pluck their lyres
    Where the green translucency beats,
And with motionless eyes at gaze
    Make minstrelsy in the streets.'

and *The Little Creature*, a piece of spellbinding incantation,
and a perfect example of de la Mare's power with words.
The poem has enormous rhythmic drive.

'Twinkum, twankum, twirlum and twitch—
My great grandam—She was a Witch.
Mouse in wainscot, Saint in niche—
My great grandam—She was a Witch;
Deadly nightshade flowers in a ditch—

My great grandam—She was a Witch;
Long though the shroud, it grows stitch by stitch—
My great grandam—She was a Witch;
Wean your weakling before you breech—
My great grandam—She was a Witch;
The fattest pig's but a double flitch—
My great grandam—She was a Witch;
Nightjars rattle, owls scritch—
My great grandam—She was a Witch.'

Down-Adown-Derry has its lost children as well, spirited away by magic and calling voices. There are wastes of snow, too, and at the end of *them*, a sorcerer waits.

Poems for Children, with the exception of some twenty new poems, is also a selection from earlier books. But it is important to the student of de la Mare's work because of its Introduction, which should be familiar to anyone interested in de la Mare as a writer for children. It examines, for one thing, the nature of poetry itself.

'Poetry indeed is not only one of the rarest, but also one of the most curious things that men make. Age cannot wither it, nor custom stale its infinite variety, and yet it depends for its very life on being remembered.'

And,

'A poem, again, read when one is young *may* seem no poem at all when one is older. Still more often, a poem when one is older may take to itself a life-givingness, a music and a depth of meaning that one never perceived in it at all when one read it as a child.'

And again,

'Yet another curious thing about poetry is the question of where it comes from. Not usually, it seems, does it spring up in the mind today out of what happened yesterday. The bee flies about among the thorn trees, but the nectar he sips must wait awhile before it becomes honey. It may be impossible for the writer of it to recollect when and where any particular poem was written, or the mood in which it was written.'

De la Mare then asks a question which he asked continually throughout his long life. What are children? He answers it as best he can by saying,

'It is the mind that most matters though that, too, has a good deal to do with the body. But whatever precisely a child may be, it is very unusual indeed for those who have become men to be able to remember precisely what it was to be one; to become, that is, in imagination, the children they actually once were.'

There then follows this wisdom,

'. . . one has only to be quiet and watchful in the company of any child . . . to become aware (though in a very cloudy and partial fashion) of the astonishingly full and vivid life it is leading—and being led by. The life, that is, of what, so to speak, is outside of itself and what is inside of itself: its body life, its mind life, and its spirit life . . . And though it doesn't appear to be usually taken into account, it is certain that children, both in mind and imagination, however little it may be apparent, are likely to be more different from one another even than men and women are different from one another.'

Most people would accept these statements without question. Our age has grown up with them, though the phrase 'however little it may be apparent' is still often forgotten. But at the time the Introduction was written it could not be said that most thinking adults *would* have accepted what de la Mare knew in his heart to be true about young children. But he lived with these ideas all his life. His very first published books were really illustrations, with slight variations, of all that he believed to be true.

The selected poems contain the old favourites. But of the new poems, there is the longish *Sam's Three Wishes*, and poems about birds, animals (and their language, in *Babel*), London, the Thames, winter, and a poem called *Snow* which gives a good idea of de la Mare's technical skill as well as his ability to describe a scene by selecting what is most significant in it.

> 'No breath of wind,
> No gleam of sun—
> Still the white snow
> Whirls softly down—
> Twig and bough
> And blade and thorn
> All in an icy quiet, forlorn.
> Whispering, rustling,
> Through the air,
> On sill and stone,
> Roof—everywhere,
> It heaps its powdery
> Crystal flakes,
> On every tree
> A mountain makes,
> Till pale and faint
> At shut of day
> Stoops from the West
> One wintry ray,
> And, feathered in fire,
> Where ghosts the moon,
> A robin shrills
> His lonely tune.'

This Year, *Next Year* was the joint effort of de la Mare and Harold Jones, the illustrator. Harold Jones drew the pictures

and de la Mare wrote verses to them. In his rhyming introduction, addressed to 'Dear Reader', de la Mare had this
to say about the illustrator,

> 'And though (I should confess betimes),
> There was no need at all for rhymes,
> 'Twas yet the more a joy to tell,
> If only in headlong doggerel,
> What rich and lively company
> His Picture-Book has been to me.'

This is the perfect, physical world of the young child. No
aspect of that absorbing world seems to be omitted. How
well de la Mare understood the active adventuring body and
mind of one who had only just left infancy behind him.

Bells and Grass has a short introduction which begins on
rather a sad note.

'. . . this little collection of rhymes will be the last of its
kind that I shall have the opportunity of making.'

Although not published until de la Mare was nearly
seventy, many of the rhymes had been written in the early
years of the century, with those of *Songs of Childhood* and
Peacock Pie, and

'. . . had had the *young* in mind . . . they had been written
by and through that self within which, in however small a
degree, there still lurked *some*thing that might merit so
precious a tribute as that of being *described* as young. It
was the self that still delighted . . . in the old folk-tales, in
the old nursery rhymes and jingles, in early memories, and
in whatever else goes with being young: whether merry or
sad, grave or gay or tender.'

Once again the old poet tries to get to the bottom of the
nature of childhood and once again he maintains '. . . that

only the rarest kind of best in anything can be good enough
for the young.' Of the rhymes themselves, some of them
describe personal memories, though most are concerned
with 'the imagined and the imaginary. The "I" in a rhyme
is not necessarily "me".'

The rhymes of *Bells and Grass* are about children (Mary,
Tom, Nicolletta, Sallie, Sambo, Miss Apathy, Master
Proud-Face), animals, birds, grown-ups (Ben Bailey, Miss
Cherry, an old sailor, a tailor, a miller). It is a happy book
with such moods and feelings as in *White*,

> 'Once was a Miller, and he would say,
> "I go as *white* as lambs in May!
> I go as white as rose on bush!
> White as the white convolvulus!"
>
> He snapped his fingers, began to sing:—
> "White, by my beard, is everything!
> Meal, and chalk, and frost, and hail;
> Clouds and surf and ships in sail.
>
> "There's nothing on earth that brighter shines
> Than daisies and pinks and columbines;
> But how about ME when moon doth show
> And mill and meadows are deep in snow!"'

Many questions are asked but few are answered. There are
hidden voices which compel one to listen but which cannot
be dismissed. Snow falls, sleep falls, stories are told, ghosts
and strangers are abroad, with a whole company of mythical
creatures, for instance, Peridarchus the Prince of Mouses
and Eenanennika the Midget. *Bells and Grass* has the same
kind of magic as *Songs of Childhood* and *Peacock Pie*, and
yet, for all the earlier rhymes, it is the book of an old
man who sees his childhood a very long way off and because this is so, conveys a more regretful note, for all the

spells, incantations and twentieth-century nursery rhymes
and jingles. Perhaps de la Mare expressed this sighing and
nostalgia most strongly in *Gone*.

> 'Where's the Queen of Sheba?
> Where King Solomon?
> Gone with Boy Blue who looks after the sheep,
> Gone and gone and gone.
>
> Lovely is the sunshine;
> Lovely is the wheat;
> Lovely the wind from out of the clouds
> Having its way with it.
>
> Rise up, Old Green-Stalks!
> Delve deep, Old Corn!
> But where's the Queen of Sheba?
> Where King Solomon?'

Most of de la Mare's poems for children, or about child-
ren, were included by him in *Collected Rhymes and Verses*,
where they are arranged under such inviting headings as
Green Grow the Rushes, O, *All Round the Town*, *Soldiers:
Sailors: Far Countries: and the Sea*, *All Creatures Great and
Small*, *Fairies: Witches: Phantoms*, *Winter and Christmas*,
Books and Stories, *Moon: and Stars: Night: And Dreams*,
Odds and Ends, *Somewhere*—over three hundred of them.
Three hundred poems. What a contribution to the poetry
of childhood! Who has matched it in range and quality?
Who has written finer poems about fairies, witches, winter,
snow, dreamland, the moon? But it is necessary to study the
earlier books in order to see how *Collected Rhymes and Verses*
came into being.

Now what does all this amount to? How important *is*
Walter de la Mare as a writer of poetry for children? Is he
unique? What chances has he of survival?

Walter de la Mare was a poet who believed in the beauty and everlastingness of the human spirit. And he saw these flashes of eternity—as Traherne, Vaughan and Wordsworth had seen them before him—at their loveliest and strongest in childhood. His poetry has, in the first place, quality of a very high and individual order, and in the second, it concerns itself with that cosmos which is essentially the cosmos of childhood. Lear and Carroll were witty poets, Wordsworth was in deadly earnest, Blake saw children as a mystic enjoys heaven, Stevenson's children were wistful or gay, Allingham's, fanciful, Christina Rossetti held hers in her arms. But Walter de la Mare wrote as if he were a child himself, as if he were *revealing* his own childhood, though with the mature gifts of the authentic poet. His children are true to childhood. They are certainly not *all* children. But they are de la Mare children. And they are alive. He was ensnared by the boy who was the fatherless de la Mare. And that child was modest, withdrawn, in close touch with terrors and splendours, never corrupted by the world, fanciful, constant. The de la Mare child has fears and uncertainties but unusual joys and pleasures. He dwells with common things but is never far in spirit from the supernatural. He is at one and the same time in an England of fields and seas, and in a Nowhere of dreams and sleep. This child is a complex being, very imaginative and always listening. De la Mare's verses and rhymes give delight because they go to the hearts of children, to the essence of childhood. As Lillian H. Smith wrote in *The Unreluctant Years*: 'It is this capacity to see "the rarest charm of familiarity in strangeness," the beauty of this earth in its relation to spiritual beauty, separated one from the other only by a veil of gossamer compounded of imagination, vision, and dream, into which beauty breaks through when we least expect it. His mastery of flexible and subtle rhythms is so deft that it is, perhaps, hardly realised.'

Few other English poets have possessed *all* these gifts, and as childhood more and more re-inherits its birthright, so will de la Mare be seen to be the rarest of them all because he trusted childhood's intuitive response. His genius was not so much in knowing by instinct, experience and observation, as in his ability to put all these into words which conveyed what he knew and felt, and yet had a divinity of their own. As he said in *Dreams*,

> 'But words are shallow, and soon
> Dreams fade that the heart once knew;
> And youth fades out in the mind,
>   In the dark eyes too.
>
> What can a tired heart say
> Which the wise of the world have made dumb?
> Save to the lonely heart of a child,
>   "Return again, come!"'

But it might be profitable to examine a couple of his poems in detail.

The Storm, which appeared in *Bells and Grass* (1941), is a good example of Walter de la Mare's method of working.

> 'First there were two of us, then there were three of us,
> Then there was one bird more,
> Four of us—wild white sea-birds,
> Treading the ocean floor;
> And the *wind* rose, and the *sea* rose,
> To the angry billows' roar—
> With one of us—two of us—three of us—four of us
> Sea-birds on the shore.
>
> Soon there were five of us, soon there were nine of us,
> And lo! in a trice sixteen!
> And the yeasty surf curdled over the sands,

The gaunt grey rocks between;
And the tempest raved, and the lightning's fire
Struck blue on the spindrift hoar—
And on four of us—ay, and on four times four of us
Sea-birds on the shore.

And our sixteen waxed to thirty-two,
And they to past three score—
A wild, white welter of winnowing wings,
And ever more and more;
And the winds lulled, and the sea went down,
And the sun streamed out on high,
Gilding the pools and the spume and the spars
'Neath the vast blue deeps of the sky;

And the isles and the bright green headlands shone,
As they'd never shone before,
Mountains and valleys of silver cloud,
Wherein to swing, sweep, soar—
A host of screeching, scolding, scrabbling
Sea-birds on the shore—
A snowy, silent, sun-washed drift
Of sea-birds on the shore.'

This has a great sense of atmosphere. Its architecture is beautifully constructed to a traditional pattern and it echoes with the most lovely sounds. First there is the cumulative effect, as the sea-birds gather. This is the first theme. The sea is calm and there are, at first, only two birds 'treading the ocean floor'. Then three, then four ('one bird more') five, nine (three times three), sixteen (four times four), then thirty-two, sixty-four ('past three score'), all worked out mathematically. Then it becomes impossible to count the birds. We are told they are a 'welter', then 'a host', and finally, a 'drift'. The precision is lost, but it is not hard to visualise what large numbers of birds there were. And, as if this is not enough, the 'welter' has to be 'a wild, white welter of winnowing wings' and the 'host', a 'host of screeching, scolding, scrabbling sea-birds' and 'the drift', 'a snowy, silent, sun-washed drift of sea-birds'.

Everything has been observed minutely and accurately assimilated. The facts are all there but they are illumined by an imagination, which knew, by instinct and training, how to present them in the most telling manner to other imaginations. Then there is the second theme of the rising storm, in counterpoint to the theme of the growing number of birds. The gulls, with the wind and rain, become indivisibly intermingled, to give an unusual mixture of sight and sound. The storm effects are obtained by the underlining of 'wind' and 'sea' in the first verse, the line 'And the yeasty surf curdled over the sands' (a clever use of the long 'e' and long 'u' sounds, and the lines,

> 'And the tempest raved, and the lightning's fire
> Struck blue on the spindrift hoar'

with the long 'a' of 'raved', and the long and short 'i's' of 'lightning' 'fire' and 'spindrift', the short and long 'u's' of 'struck' and 'blue', and then the glorious opening out of the two lines with the long 'o' of 'hoar' at the end). There are echoes of all these sounds in the third verse, with 'lulled', 'down', 'pools' and 'spume'. And the use of the word 'spindrift' instead of 'spray' gives a delightful shock of surprise at the point of the poem where it appears.

As the numbers of birds grow, so the force of the storm slackens. But with the dying away of the storm, so the noise of the birds increases. The sun shines brightly on 'the isles', 'the bright green headlands', the silver clouds ride 'mountains and valleys', but the birds are 'screeching, scolding, scrabbling'. And then the vowel sounds change to convey

calm and peace at the closing of the poem, 'A snowy, silent
sun-washed drift of sea-birds on the shore'. It is a splendid
use of language, Tennysonian in its colour, with clever
variations of movement. The poem has many contrasts,
storm with *calm*, *one bird* with *sixty-four birds*, *noise of storm*
with *quiet of birds*, *noise of birds* with *quiet of sea and shore*,
birds at rest with *birds who swing*, *'sweep and soar'*. The
poem, though a unity, is episodic. It has its pauses (one in
the first verse after 'roar', one in the second after 'hoar', one
in the third, after 'score', and two in the fourth, after 'soar'
and 'shore'—all, it is to be observed, heralded by the same
rhyming sound) and it has its enormous driving movement,
made possible by the use of 'and' at the beginnings of no
less than eleven lines.

How perfect was the ear that could deal so ingeniously
with alliteration, assonance and dissonance. The sound of
's' or 'ch' or the soft 'c', is used seventy-five times in these
four verses, and the sound of 'w', twenty times. The rhyming pattern is very simple. Only three sounds are used, the
long 'o', the long 'e' and the long 'i'. And yet the interest is
kept up for the thirty-two lines of the poem.

The Storm is a fine conception, a perfect picture, very
kind on the ear and pleasant to the eye. It is the poem of a
word-musician with the keenest of eyes. But it is something
more than a brilliant piece of clean-cut description. It has
its own inner peace and life and freshness of light, which are
noble and uplifting.

Now Silent Falls is a poem of a different order, but it is
clearly a poem written by the same master hand.

> 'Now silent falls the clacking mill;
> Sweet—sweeter smells the briar;
> The dew wells big on bud and twig;
> The glow-worm's wrapt in fire.

Then sing, lully, lullay, with me,
And softly, lill-lall-lo, love,
'Tis high time, and wild time,
And no time, no, love!

The Western sky has vailed her rose;
The night-wind to the willow
Sigheth, "Now lovely, lean thy head,
Thy tresses be my pillow!"

Then sing, lully, lullay, with me,
And softly, lill-lall-lo, love,
'Tis high time, and wild time,
And no time, no, love!

Cries in the brake, bells in the sea;
The moon o'er moor and mountain
Cruddles her light from height to height,
Bedazzles pool and fountain.

Leap, fox; hoot, owl; wail, warbler sweet:
'Tis midnight now's a-brewing;
The fairy mob is all abroad,
And witches at their wooing. . . .

Then sing, lully, lullay, with me,
And softly, lill-lall-lo, love,
'Tis high time, and wild time,
And no time, no, love.'

It is a song from de la Mare's only play, *Crossings* (1923),
where it is sung (to music by C. Armstrong Gibbs) by Sallie
Wildersham for her baby sister, Ann, in their Bayswater
house on a foggy, December day at the beginning of the
century. It is, in fact, a lullaby for winter evenings, with its
remembrances of summer dusks. Each of its seven verses is
in ballad metre, and its form is binary (with variation), e.g.

A.B., A.B., A.A.B., that is, four different verses, and a
refrain repeated three times. This simplicity conjures up
magical sounds (sometimes by the very absence of them) and
tender, limpid movement. And the whole is bathed in soft
moonlight. The rise and fall of the various sounds is most
appealing, a fine example of how a poet can change pitch
when he wishes to convey an effect. For instance the first
verse has:

'Now silent falls the clacking mill; (ow, long 'i', aw,
                                    long 'a', short 'i')
Sweet—sweeter smells the briar; (long 'e', short 'e', long 'i')
The dew wells big on bud and twig; (long 'u', short 'e',
                                    short 'i', short 'u',
                                    long 'a', short 'i')
The glow-worm's wrapt in fire.' (long 'o', er, long 'a',
                                    short 'i', long 'i')

And so it goes on, falling very happily on the ear. The
letter 'w' is used, on ten occasions, to induce sleep—*wells*,
glow-worms, *wrapt*, *wild*, *western*, *night-wind*, *willows*,
warbler, *witches*, *wooing*. The letter 'b' is used on eight
occasions, to produce much the same sensation—*briar*, *bud*,
brake, *bells*, *bedazzles*, *brewing*, *mob*, *abroad*. There is the
exciting use of 'wells' in the first verse ('The dew wells'), of
'vailed' in the second ('vailed her rose;'—meaning that the
sky has let her rose colour fall), of 'cruddles' (an obsolete
word meaning 'curdles'), in the third line of the fifth verse,
of 'mob' in association with 'fairy' in the third line of the
sixth verse.

The refrain is a magical amalgam of sound, rhythm and
meaning. Every word counts. 'Sing' goes with 'softly',
'lully' broadens to 'lullay', and then changes to 'lill-lall-lo',
and finishes with 'wild' and 'love'. There is the long 'i'
chiming in 'high time, and wild time'. There are eleven

commas in the four short lines of this refrain. These give the pauses and, as a result, a very subtle rocking rhythm, made even more telling by the syncopation of 'lill-lall-lo' and the second 'no' in the last line (sprung rhythm, in fact). The choice of 'high', 'wild', and 'no' in connection with 'time' is delightful; 'high' time (quite time to go to sleep), 'wild' time (when time finishes as an exact measurement with the coming of dusk and dream) and the sheer inspiration of 'no' time (time finishes, there is no longer any time, emphasised by the second 'no').

In the play, the stage directions immediately before the lullaby is sung, read, 'She kneels down for a moment or two beside Ann, then seats herself at the spinet. The tinkling keys sound like a faintly cantankerous voice reawaked out of a quiet, centuries old.' It is as if the lullaby had not only sent the little girl off to sleep but, in true de la Mare fashion, had been heard by spirits *somewhere* and had called them up out of their silences. As the second sister, Frances, says when the song is finished, 'You can have no notion how that tinkle-tinkle-tankle skips echoing up into those hundreds of little old empty rooms and corridors—empty and empty. Sleep? not me! Dream *this* side, say I,—when you can.'

Now Silent Falls is a poem of dreams 'this side', of echoes, of the *sounds* of the 'clacking mill', the sighing night wind, the 'cries in the brake', bells sunk beneath the sea, of hooting owls and wailing warblers. And it is a poem of *sights*, of dew 'on bud and twig', of glow-worm, roseate sky, moon, pool, fountain, leaping fox, fairies and witches. And the whole poem is suffused with just one *smell*—the sweet briar.

v. The Storyteller

' "Well, you see Letitia, a story ought
to be like a piece of embroidery: it ought
to have a beginning and a middle and an
end. It ought to be like a whiting with its
tail in its mouth." '

from Walter de la Mare's
story *Old Joe*

And so to de la Mare as a storyteller.

His longest story, *The Three Royal Monkeys* (originally
known as *The Three Mulla-Mulgars*), is his prose masterpiece. It is one of the most poetical tales ever written for
children. It was, in fact, composed for, and read aloud to,
de la Mare's four children. But its qualities have not yet
been fully recognised, largely because it is a book to be best
enjoyed by grown-up children who have retained their
innocence, or by young children who can have it read to
them by such grown-ups. It is an enchanting allegorical
romance, a magical mixture of realism and fantasy. The royal
monkeys are Thumb, Thimble and Nod, living 'on the
borders of the Forest of Munza-Mulgar'. Their father,
Seelem, a Prince of the Valleys of Tishnar, is exiled from his
home. He sets out one day to return to the land of his fathers,
to be followed soon by his three sons. Before they reach
Tishnar they have the most exciting adventures and meet a
number of extraordinary animals and people, including
Andy Battle, a shipwrecked English sailor. There are times
when all seems lost but they have a 'wonderstone' with them
which never lets them down. Certainly the brave little Nod

never gives in. *The Three Royal Monkeys* is a lovely, happy story, honest and tender. Over it there rests the crispness of winter in the mountain lands of the tropics, and it is lit by the strange dawns of Tartary. It is an epic, in its way, a true picture of human life, full of love of mankind, for all that its characters are animals. It is not only an exciting tale, brilliantly related, but it is also full of de la Mare invented names—Assasimmon, Sevveras, Arakkaboa, Oomgar-Nuggas, and has wonderful descriptions of scenery, many surprises and a great sense of expectancy. There are many passages as beautiful as,

'Over the swamp stood a shaving of moon, clear as a bow of silver. And all about, on every twig, on every thorn, and leaf, and pebble; all along the nine-foot grasses, on every cushion and touch of bark, even on the walls of their hut, lay this spangling fiery meal of Tishnar—frost. He called his brothers. Their breath stood round them like smoke. They stared and snuffed, they coughed in the cold air. Never, since birds wore feathers—never had hoar-frost glittered on Munza-Mulgar before.'

Miss Jemima, the first short story that de la Mare published as a separate book, is the tale of a solitary child, as told by that child when she has become a grandmother, to her grandchild. Miss Jemima is a sadistic housekeeper who had made the child's life unbearable while her mother was in India. The story has the usual de la Mare elements—a church, a graveyard, a lonely house, and a fairy—and a great feeling for the atmosphere of the occult. This little, powerful tale is concerned to a large extent with a remark made by the granny,

'... from old fairy-tales I have got to believe that human children should be taken away to quite a different world from this—a country of enchantment.'

WALTER DE LA MARE

And here we are reminded of Tishnar, or of Tartary. The child runs away, is reunited with her mother, and all ends well.

Miss Jemima is one of the twelve original stories in the collection called *Broomsticks*. The others are *Pigtails Limited*, *The Dutch Cheese*, *The Thief*, *Broomsticks*, *Lucy*, *A Nose*, *The Three Sleeping Boys of Warwickshire*, *The Lovely Myfanwy*, *Alice's Godmother*, *Maria-Fly*, and *Visitors*. These stories are full of an unearthly stillness. In each of them—and all have scenes in strange houses—there is the curious feeling that something is about to happen. It does not always happen, but a hovering between the known and the unknown, where everyone is either very young or very old, where most of the situations are more than a little odd, gives the stories their individual quality.

The Thief, with a mid-Victorian, London background (de la Mare knew his City well, and at first hand), is the tale of a rich unhappy, professional burglar who wanted a wife.

Miss Chauncey, aged sixty (and no writer understood old ladies better than de la Mare), living in her remote, ugly house on a moor, is devoted to her cat, Sam, in *Broomsticks*, the title story. This is a story of witchcraft. Sam becomes a witch's familiar, riding on her broomstick by night. His mistress's love is not enough to hold him. Eventually Sam vanishes and is never seen again, a 'strange, deluded animal'.

In *Lucy* there are three spinster sisters, Euphemia, Tabitha and Jean Elspeth MacKnackery (what names!) who live in a ruined house. Lucy is an imagined, phantom friend. The sisters are wealthy to begin with but lose their fortunes. Euphemia dies and the other two have to leave their home. Jean Elspeth, when she is a very old woman, and wearing a mantle that had once belonged to Euphemia, pays a visit to her former home, now decaying and neglected.

'. . . and then by chance, in that deep hush, her eyes wandered to the surface of the water at her feet, and there fixed themselves, her whole mind in a sudden confusion. For by some strange freak of the cheating dusk, she saw gazing back at her from under a squat old crape bonnet, with Euphemia's cast-off beaded mantle on the shoulders beneath it, a face not in the least like that of the little old woman inside them, but a face, fair and smiling, as of one eternally young and happy and blessed—Lucy's. She gazed and gazed, in the darkening evening. A peace beyond understanding comforted her spirit. It was by far the oddest thing that had ever happened to Jean Elspeth in all the eighty years of her odd long life on earth.'

The Three Sleeping Boys of Warwickshire is one of the most enchanting stories de la Mare ever wrote for children. It is a diaphanous, dreamy, eighteenth century tale of magic, of Jeremy Nollykins the chimney-sweep, and his apprentices, Tom, Dick and Harry. Their shadow-shapes (or ghosts) are captivated by the music of *Girls and Boys Come Out to Play*. Each night when they hear it, they come from their beds to join the other sleeping children of the town. The hateful Noll watches all this and is determined to put an end to it. He consults a witch who tells him how to stop boys' ghosts getting out at night.

' "Waken a sleeper", she told him, "before his dream-shape can get back into his mortal frame, it's as like as not to be sudden death. But if you just keep the dream-shape out without rousing his sleeping body, then he will for ever more be your slave, and will never grow any older. And what keeps a human's dream-shape out—or animal's either for that matter—" she said, "is a love-knot twist of steel or a

horseshoe upside down, or a twisted wreath of elder and
ash fastened up with an iron nail over the keyhole—and
every window shut. Brick walls and stone and wood are
nothing to such wanderers. But they can't abide iron." '

The terrible result of these machinations is that the boys
fall into a trance, and are then exhibited, at sixpence a time,
in Warwick Museum. They sleep on for fifty-three years.
One day the curator's pretty niece opens the case where they
are lying and,

'... kissed the slumbering creatures on their stone-cold
mouths. And then a terrible sharp crash of glass. And out
pell-mell came rushing our three young friends, the
chimney-sweeps, their dream-shapes home at last.

'Now Old Nollykins by this time had long been laid in
his grave. So even if he had been able to catch them, Tom,
Dick, and Harry would have swept no more chimneys for
him. Nor could even the New Mayor manage to catch them;
nor even the complete Town Council, nor the Town Crier,
though he cried twice a day to the end of the year: "O-yess!
O-yess!! O-yess!!! Lost, stolen, or strayed: the Three
All-famous and Notorious Sleeping Boys of Warwickshire."
Nor even the Lord Lieutenant, nor the mighty Earl.'

Few children will be able to resist this story, full of such
poetry, wisdom and ecstasy.

Maria-Fly is a story of the minute, a delicate study of a
small, but very significant, incident in the day of an infant.
Maria saw a single—almost a solitary—fly and with such
intensity that she 'seemed almost to have *become* the fly—
"Maria-Fly".' So terrific was this experience that she just
had to tell somebody about it. She did so to a succession of
people—Mrs Poulton, the cook, Mr Kittleson, a clergyman,
Miss Salmon, a seamstress, her father, Mr Pratt, the
gardener, and Job, the gardener's boy—all typical, mid-

Victorian characters. But she gets little satisfaction from any of them, since none seem to be impressed by *her* stupendous piece of observation. Walter de la Mare gets right inside the mind and feelings of Maria. The fly at last forgotten,

'. . . she hopped down suddenly out of the arbour, almost as lightly as a thin-legged bird herself, and was off, flying over the emerald green grass into the burning delightful sunshine without in the least knowing why, or where to.'

The last story in the *Broomsticks* collection, *Visitors*, is the morbid tale of Tom Nevis, an introspective boy with a shrunken arm. We are introduced to his nurse, Alice Jenkins, we learn about his dead sister, Emily, and then two strange birds fly into the story; Tom sees them after he has been to Emily's grave. They are as white as snow as they float on a pool. He is fascinated by them. So much so that they become an obsession. He tells Alice (now married) about them, which leads her to say:

' "Of course they were real. Or else"—she gave a little gentle laugh—"or else, why you and me would be just talking about ghost birds? What I mean is that it doesn't follow even if they *was* real that they didn't mean something else too. I don't mean exactly that such things do mean anything else, but only, so to speak, *seem* that they do." '

Old Joe, the fourteenth story for, or about, children, which de la Mare published separately, is an excellent example of one of his favourite technical devices (used before in *Miss Jemima*, for instance). An elderly person tells a child the story of something that happened in his childhood. In this case, old Mr Bolsover tells his young niece, Letitia, of how, when he was ten, he 'used frequently to stay with an old friend of my mother's—your grandmother's, that is—whose name was Mrs Lumb.' He always thoroughly enjoyed himself in her old house and in the surrounding countryside where he looked for rare birds. And one day he came across a scarecrow, Old Joe, 'an antiquated hodmadod'. The boy felt that he had become a part of the hodmadod; then he became aware of a fairy who had been watching him and with whom he fell in love. At last he saw her:

' "... I recall her at this moment ... as if she were veiled about with a haze like that of a full moon—like bluebells at a little distance in a dingle of a wood. That may or may not be, but I quite clearly saw her face, for I was staring steadily into her eyes. They too were blue, like the blue of flames in a wood fire, specially when there is salt in it, or the wood has come from some old ship, with copper in it. Her hair was hanging on either side her head in a long strand from brow to chin, and down the narrow shoulder. All else in the world I had completely forgotten. I was alone, an ugly small awkward human animal looking, as if into a dream, into those strange unearthly eyes." '

So much, then for the early stories.

With *Told Again* Walter de la Mare began the series of imaginative retellings of old tales which he was to transform with his poet's language. He reshaped them without destroying their original force, improving, at times, upon earlier versions. The nineteen stories he retold were taken from Aesop, Perrault, Grimm and English folk-lore, and included *Dick Whittington*, *Cinderella*, *Little Red Riding-Hood*, *Jack and the Beanstalk*, *Bluebeard*, *Snow White*, *Rumpelstiltskin* and *The Sleeping Beauty*. Not all were fairy stories. Some were about animals. Others told of the success which came to the youngest (and generally the most put-upon) son of the family, others were 'magic' stories with princes, princesses, castles, ogres, giants, dwarfs, journeyings, fortunes made and fortunes lost, the biter bit. De la Mare's gifts as a storyteller enabled him to intensify the atmosphere of all these. In each case he added dialogue, many charming backcloth descriptions, and, in so doing, 'filled out' the tales. It is often said that it is the duty of parents and teachers to introduce their children to the great heritage of English literature. *Told Again* contains some of this heritage as presented by a master, as does *Animal Stories* to a still greater extent. A child brought up on these undying traditional stories is fortunate indeed.

Told Again was followed by more retellings, this time of *Stories from the Bible*, which has remained one of de la Mare's most popular collections. A short Introduction outlines the scope of the book:

'The stories contained in this volume are versions of but a few of the narratives related in the first nine books of the Old Testament of the Bible.'

De la Mare then dealt with the problems of translation and of retelling, made an apology for the task to be undertaken, and ended characteristically,

'If, in spite of all its defects and shortcomings, this book persuades any of its young readers to return to the inexhaustible well-spring from which it came, it will have amply fulfilled its purpose.'

The stories chosen were *The Garden of Eden*, *The Flood*, *Joseph*, *Moses*, *The Wilderness*, *Samson*, *Samuel*, *Saul* and *David*. An American critic, Edward Wagenknecht, wrote in 1950,

'In *Stories from the Bible* he produced the only modern paraphrase I know that does not travesty its original. If he could only be persuaded to apply the same method to the Gospels—and it is I think, an excessive sense of reverence that has hitherto restrained him—I am fully persuaded that he could produce the best literary Life of Christ that has ever been written.'

But that Walter de la Mare never did. However, the re-tellings of the Old Testament stories certainly add something to our reverence and a great deal to our imaginative grasp of God's purposes for mankind. The stories are most suitable, perhaps, for young adolescents.

There are seven stories in *The Lord Fish* collection. Illustrated by Rex Whistler, it contains five of his sublimest tales, *The Lord Fish, The Jacket, Dick and the Beanstalk, The Old Lion*, and *Sambo and the Snow Mountains*; the other two are *A Penny A Day* and *Hodmadod* (the new title for *Old Joe*). *The Lord Fish* is de la Mare's most ambitious story. It tells of the amazing adventures of lazy John Cobbler of Tussock in Wiltshire—a young fisherman who fished morning, noon and night. One day, John comes upon a mysterious, solitary house, catches a pike from a stream that runs near it and finds a key inside the fish. Eventually he is caught by the great Lord Fish and kept by him, in a fish-like state, in his stone house. John Cobbler is in grave danger of being eaten but, through the good offices of the maid who is the Lord Fish's servant, gains his freedom, to discover a casket which is to make his fortune. There is some dazzling writing in this story. There are many passages like this one, for instance:

'While yet next morning the eastern sky was pale blue with the early light of dawn, wherein tiny clouds like a shoal of silver fishes were quietly drifting on—before, that is, the flaming sun had risen, John was posting along out of Tussock with his rod and tackle and battered old creel, and a hunk of bread and cheese tied up in a red spotted handkerchief. There was not a soul to be seen. Every blind was down; the chimneys were empty of smoke; the whole village was still snoring. He whistled as he walked, and every now and again took a look at the sky. That vanishing fleecy drift of silver fishes might mean wind, and from the south, he thought. He plodded along to such good purpose, and without meeting a soul except a shepherd with his sheep and dog and an urchin driving a handful of cows—for these were solitary parts—that he came to the wall while it was still morning, and a morning as fresh and green as even England can show.'

The Jacket is another tale of magic—of a magic jacket, in fact—of an admiral and a boy who was a pavement artist. Here we have the contrast between the very old and the very young again. It is a fine study of motives and character, and so is *Dick and the Beanstalk*, an amusing, imaginative tale, beginning where *Jack and the Beanstalk* had left off.

The Old Lion is a tender, glowing story and a good example of de la Mare's instinctive understanding of the feelings of animals and the relationship between them and those humans who try to get closer to them. He gets right inside the heart and mind of Mr Bumps, the monkey, wins our pity and makes us ashamed that a living creature of such intelligence has to be humiliated.

The last story of this collection, *Sambo and the Snow Mountains*, is a gem. It tells of 'the othere worlde', of Sambo's efforts to make himself white (he was a Negro of darkest hue) and of his strange meeting with Miss Bleech (what a name!) in the Snow Mountains. Sambo tended the old lady until she died, to find that she had left him her fortune.

'And yet, in the years that followed, as he lived on at peace in his mansion in the Snow Mountains, gazing out of his window—a thing he never wearied of—a strange craving at

164

times would creep into Sambo's mind. And the fear would take him that Satan was nearing again. At this he would steal to his looking glass, and confront, on and on, that speckless face of chalk from eyes as motionless and dark as basalt.

' "O but for a moment," a voice would cry out in him as if from the very recesses of his being, "O but for a moment, to be black again!" And always, to silence the voice, Sambo would pick a few snow-flowers and go down and lay them on his old friend's grave. There he would stay for a few moments, alone in the valley, looking up at the tranquil hills; and then, slowly and solemnly shaking his white-washed head, would return again—comforted.'

Walter de la Mare wrote no more original stories for children after these twenty. *The Old Lion* re-appeared in 1942 as *Mr Bumps and His Monkey*, illustrated by Dorothy Lathrop. The collection, called *The Old Lion*, which appeared in the same year, had *that* story, *Maria-Fly*, *The Lord Fish*, and *Sambo and the Snow Mountains*. *The Magic Jacket*, of 1944, had *The Magic Jacket* (= *The Jacket*), *Miss Jemima*, *Dick and the Beanstalk* and *The Riddle* (originally in a collection for adults, but a compelling story about children). *The Scarecrow*, of 1945, had *The Scarecrow of Hodmadod* (= *Hodmadod* = *Old Joe*), *The Lovely Myfanwy*, *Broomsticks* and *Visitors*.

And finally, the *Collected Stories for Children* of 1947, had the following seventeen:

> *Dick and The Beanstalk*
> *The Dutch Cheese*
> *A Penny A Day*
> *The Scarecrow*
> *The Three Sleeping Boys of Warwickshire*
> *The Lovely Myfanwy*

Lucy
Miss Jemima
The Magic Jacket
The Lord Fish
The Old Lion
Broomsticks
Alice's Godmother
Maria-Fly
Visitors
Sambo and the Snow Mountains
The Riddle

It was this collection which was awarded the Carnegie Medal of The Library Association. The writer of *Chosen for Children* (published by the Library Association) said,

'Walter de la Mare's *Collected Stories for Children* was a new book of 1947 in a bibliographical, not a literary, sense. Each of the seventeen tales had been printed before, one as long ago as 1900. The publication of the *Collected Stories* offered, however, the last opportunity for the Library Association to recognise the unique contribution which Walter de la Mare had made to children's literature. For nearly half a century he had devoted to children the same qualities which had made him so distinctive and memorable a writer of prose and verse for adults. No other writer had given so generously of his best to children, so that it was impossible to say that *Peacock Pie* was inferior to *Motley* or *The Three Mulla-Mulgars* to *The Return*. It was therefore a cause for rejoicing that the Library Association had interpreted in so liberal a spirit its regulations by honouring a book which so richly summed up a life devoted to the delight and the understanding of children. . . . *Collected Stories for Children* is representative of the creative work of forty years. It has, nevertheless, a remarkable unity in mood and style, however diverse the subject-matter and the treatment. . . . Walter de la Mare is in all these stories a fine craftsman and a sensitive observer. He never condescends to his readers, and never forgets that, of all the wonders in the world which he explores so profoundly and so sadly, the greatest wonder is the child's fresh and penetrating vision.'

Perhaps the most striking thing about Walter de la Mare's fairy tales is that they are the work of a mystic and not of a sceptic.

There remain *Animal Stories*, described as 'chosen, arranged, and in some part re-written, by Walter de la Mare'. There are forty-two stories and forty-six rhymes. Of the forty-two stories, one, *The Lord Fish*, is the original story already discussed, and three, *Whittington and His Cat*, *The Hare and the Hedgehog* and *The Wolf and the Fox*, are revisions of stories, with the same titles, which had been included in the earlier collection, *Told Again*; one, *All Gone*, had appeared in a previous book, *Readings*, though with a different title. The other stories come from various sources. Two of them, *A Sailor's Yarn* and *The Seal Man*, were written by John Masefield. Most of the rest are traditional in origin. De la Mare included such favourites as *The Three Little Pigs*, *The Three Bears*, and *Puss in Boots*, and several, not so well-known, or only half-remembered. Of the forty-six rhymes, one, *The Hare*, came from *Songs of Childhood*; another, *Tony O'*, was by a writer called Colin Francis, and the rest, traditional songs and rhymes from all parts of the British Isles, with a few short poems by Shakespeare, Ravenscroft and Coleridge.

The collection is so arranged that each story is preceded by a rhyme. *Animal Stories* is an exciting and scholarly anthology giving further proof of de la Mare's gifts as an editor. It is a storehouse of knowledge and a treasure house of delight. No child brought up on it would be without his heritage of traditional animal literature. Hardly an animal is excluded, but it is the homely ones which play the leading parts—hare, hedgehog, mouse, frog, pig, cat, dog, chicken, fox, goose, ox, ass, sparrow—and the human beings take second place and, more often than not, animals bring *them* their good fortune.

De la Mare wrote a very informative essay on animal stories as an introduction to the book. He examines the old tales, rhymes and jingles, and talks about the history of their literature and the books where he had found them, though many 'were either said or told to me, or read to me, for the first time when I was a small child'. And he has this to say in connection with children,

'My private impression, for what it is worth, is that in mind and spirit we are most of us born (as it were) at the age at which for the rest of our lives we are likely to remain.'

And about the stories,

'These are tales of the *imagination* . . . whether we delight in them or not, depends, then, on how much imagination we have ourselves.'

He goes into the subject very thoroughly, discusses nursery tales, fairy tales, myths, and sagas of trial and adventure, and then attempts to examine the natures of animals as regards their instinct and intelligence (quoting from his own tale, *Broomsticks*, to prove a point about the behaviour of cats). De la Mare makes his own position very clear about animals.

'Whatever our own views concerning God's living, mysterious and wonderful creatures may be, there is no doubt what the folk, the tellers of these old tales thought and felt about them. The animals in them, the birds, even the bees and the ants, each in its own kind, act very much as humans would if they were in their skins.'

This essay about animal lore is one of the best of its kind in the language and no one who wishes to read stories about animals should miss it. Later on, in 1949, in his introduction to Miss M. M. Johnson's anthology, *These Also*, de la Mare was to write,

'Her ardent concern is with the living creatures of every estate that during our own brief stay on this earth share it with us—their life, wonder, mystery and benefactions. It is for her an earth whose blissful nucleus once was Eden, and may some day be the New Jerusalem. It was a paradise from which Adam in his divinely-given sovereignty "fell", and so became at length a dictator corrupted by power. She is no less assured that these creatures not only enliven and enrich but that they "glorify" the earth; that few of us, whether out of indifference or insensitiveness, realise this; that our insight into their nature and faculties falls far short even of our own innate gifts, and certainly of theirs; and that our usual treatment of them is not only against their interests and our own, but shallow and dead-alive. "Am I my brother's keeper?" "Yes," she replies, "and also your brother the ass's, and the skylark's. But not in a cage." '

Walter de la Mare's contribution to children's prose literature, therefore, consists of twenty original stories and sixty retellings. This is a considerable contribution when its quality and range are remembered and also that he was primarily a poet whose chief work for children was in the medium most natural to him.

His fairy play, *Crossings*, is a failure. A few of the songs, set to music by Armstrong Gibbs, will live on, but the play is a box of rather obvious tricks. We are introduced to a lonely house, an odd aunt, the moon, the snow, voices in the wind, a family of bewitched children, fairies, and some unlikely tradesmen. Some of the dialogue is very sentimental. We would expect de la Mare's world to be unreal, but the unreality of *Crossings* is unconvincing.

VI. The Editor

Now for a few of the anthologies.

Tom Tiddler's Ground was first published in 1931, with Bewick woodcut decorations and the rhymes which de la Mare so wisely chose, and annotated, for young people though they gave 'only a glimpse of the great feast of English poetry'. It was reissued in 1961 with new illustrations. The brief introduction to the anthology gives good advice to children, and to their teachers, about the reading of poetry,

'We can . . . and particularly when we are young, delight in the sound of the words of a poem, immensely enjoy them —the music and rhythm and lilt, feel its enchantment and treasure it in memory, without realising its *full* meaning.'

And what good sense is contained in the remark:

'It is best to find your way in a poem for yourself.'

Come Hither, described as 'A collection of rhymes and poems for the young of all ages,' is still one of the finest of all anthologies, whether for old or young. First published in 1923, it was revised and enlarged in 1928 and reissued in 1960 with new illustrations. The 483 poems by 260 poets, both known and unknown, and spanning 600 years, are introduced by an allegorical story of how the book came into being. A boy, Simon, on his way to a place called East Dene, comes across an 'old stone house in the hollow' called THREA (Earth) and eventually meets Miss Taroone (= Nature) and her relative, Nahum Taroone (= Human Nature). Simon explores the strange house and Nahum's cases of books and discovers (?) the poems, which are to make up *Come Hither*, in a special book *Theothaworldie*,

'. . . certain rhymes and poems affected my mind when I was young, and continue to do so now I am old. To these (and a few bits of prose) which I chose from Mr Nahum, I added others afterwards, and they are in this book too. All of them are in English.'

The poems (including two rhymes by de la Mare hidden, almost anonymously, in the notes) are followed by three hundred pages of illuminating, evocative and scholarly remarks on the books, showing an amazing knowledge of poetry and great feeling for its inner heart. De la Mare divided the book into sections, to cover the world of childhood (one of his favourite devices as an editor). These are *Morning And May*, *Mother*, *Home and Sweetheart*, *Feasts: Fairs: Beggars: Gypsies*, *Elphin: Ouph: Fay*, *Beasts of the Field: Fowls of the Air*, *Summer: Greenwood: Solitude*, *War*, *Dance*, *Music And Bells*, *Autumn Leaves: Winter Snow*, '*Like Stars upon Some Gloomy Grove*', *Far*, '*Lily Bright and Shine-A*', '*Echo Then Shall Again, Tell Her I Follow*', *Old Tales and Balladry*, *Evening and Dream*, *The Garden*. The pattern of *Come Hither* has often been imitated but, as a comprehensive collection of poems for children, it has yet to be superseded. It is very highly thought of in America.

Early One Morning in the Spring is also comprehensive. It is an informed and authoritative book consisting of 'Chapters on Children and on Childhood as it is revealed in particular in Early Memories and in Early Writings.' These chapters are concerned with such aspects of childhood as intelligence, happiness, memory, play, learning, food, clothes, and people. The Early Writings are taken from journals, letters, stories and verse. A galaxy of geniuses is introduced, including Bacon, Hazlitt, Thackeray, Henry James and Mozart. It is difficult to describe a book of this nature adequately, for it is so full of information and wisdom gathered from first-hand experience, personal memories and wide reading. The book has to be read from cover to cover and its comments savoured to the full. A brief introduction describes the attitudes of adults to babies, childhood and young animals. De la Mare talks of,

'. . . the various degrees of approach between the grown-up and the young, from sheer insensitiveness to the rarest insight and understanding. And yet I believe those who can win nearest to childhood, and be wholly at peace, at liberty, and at ease in its company, would be the first to acknowledge that they can never get nearer than very near, never actually *there*.'

Early One Morning in the Spring is a model of sympathy and understanding. De la Mare himself certainly got 'very near'. It establishes him as a writer for children who knew about children and from many sources, who had studied childhood in most of its aspects. It is a wonderful source book, illumined by the poetry of de la Mare's writing.

VII. Conclusion

This, then, is the evidence upon which rests the claim for Walter de la Mare that he was a superb writer for children. The comments made about his work in this monograph are but slight and the quotations from his various books mere peep-holes into his strange but fascinating kingdom. For those who want further proof of his genius there are the poems, stories and other writings themselves, in all their completeness, each one of which demands careful reading and thoughtful study. Walter de la Mare was a writer whose voice was so personal and whose style so wonderfully matched that voice, they cannot accurately be torn apart. But the craftsmanship is there as well as the shining quality and unearthly loveliness; the glow of the fire as well as the fire itself. His poems, more so than his stories, are a part of the canon of children's literature, and will remain so. These poems see beauty on earth, are aware that beauty vanishes, but that its recognition, however minute, is sufficient to give a glimpse through a few cracks in Time into eternity. These poems are 'shoots of everlastingness'. And yet Walter de la Mare's full stature has yet to be acknowledged, even in his own country, and this perhaps, because he so often wrote of lonely mysteries. He was, too, a pioneer born into an age when writing for children was at a low ebb. Nevertheless it would be a mistake to think that he was only a poet who thought in terms of beauty. He was too forthright a character for that. Neither would it be proper to isolate what he wrote for children from the main body of his work. He wrote intuitively as if he were a child with a child's vision and willingness to believe, and for those who, besides children, retain in their spirits some of the genuine characteristics of children. We turn to Walter de la Mare, English poet and storyteller, for delight, innocence, perfect harmony of sound and colour, enormous variety of rhythms and poetic structure. We soar with him on the wings of imagination. He has also his distant echoes and inexplicable shadows. But, above all, he had a devotion to his art which was never obscured and which, in the end, is recognised as being purely religious, because it rejoiced in all creation, and hallowed its Creator.

SELECT BIBLIOGRAPHY

Select Bibliography

BOOKS ABOUT WALTER DE LA MARE

Walter de la Mare. A Critical Study by Forrest Reid. (Faber, 1929)
Tribute to Walter de la Mare on His 75th Birthday. (Faber, 1948)
Walter de la Mare. A Study of His Poetry by H. C. Duffin. (Sidgwick & Jackson, 1949)
Walter de la Mare by Kenneth Hopkins. (Published for The British Council and The National Book League by Longmans, 1953)
Walter de la Mare (A Checklist prepared on the occasion of an Exhibition of his Books and Manuscripts at the National Book League) by Leonard Clark. (Cambridge University Press, 1956)
Tea with Walter de la Mare by Sir Russell Brain. (Faber, 1957)

BOOKS BY WALTER DE LA MARE AS A WRITER FOR, AND ABOUT, CHILDREN

POETRY

Songs of Childhood. (Longmans, 1902. Now published by Faber)
A Child's Day. (Constable, 1912)
Peacock Pie. (Constable, 1913. Now published by Faber)
Down-Adown-Derry. (Constable, 1922)
Stuff and Nonsense. (Constable, 1927. Then published by Faber)
Poems for Children. (Constable, 1930)
This Year, Next Year. (Faber, 1937)
Bells and Grass. (Faber, 1941)
Collected Rhymes and Verses. (Faber, 1944)
Selected Stories and Verses. (Edited by Eleanor Graham) (Penguin Books, 1952)
Complete Poems of Walter de la Mare. (Edited by Leonard Clark) (Faber, 1968)

* = in print

PLAY

Crossings. (Beaumont Press, 1921. Faber, 1942)

STORIES

The Three Mulla-Mulgars. (Duckworth, 1910. Now published by Faber as *The Three Royal Monkeys*)

Story and Rhyme. (Dent, 1921)

Miss Jemima. (Blackwell, 1925)

Broomsticks and Other Tales. (Constable, 1925)

Lucy. (Blackwell, 1927)

Old Joe. (Blackwell, 1927)

Told Again. (Blackwell, 1927. Now published by Faber as *Tales Told Again*)

Stories from the Bible. (Faber and Gwyer, 1929. Four of the stories, Joseph, Samuel, Moses, and Saul, are now published by Faber, and illustrated by Edward Ardizzone)

The Lord Fish and Other Tales. (Faber, 1933)

Animal Stories. (Faber, 1939)

The Old Lion and Other Stories. (Faber, 1942)

The Magic Jacket and Other Stories. (Faber, 1944)

The Scarecrow and Other Stories. (Faber, 1945)

The Dutch Cheese and Other Stories. (Faber, 1946)

Collected Stories for Children. (Faber, 1947)

GRAMOPHONE RECORDS

| Columbia D.X.1905 | Robert Harris and Jill Balcon | *All That's Past* *Thou Art My Long Lost Peace* *The Scribe* *Farewell* *Nostalgia* *The Forest* *Autumn* *It Was the Last Time He Was Seen* |

* = in print

Columbia D.X.1884	Robert Harris	*Arabia*
		Haunted
		No Comfort
		Sam
		Song of the Shadows
		Nod
		Song of the Mad Prince
Philips crb.1002	Norman Shelley and Mary O'Farrell	*Tartary*
		Many a Mickle
		Five Eyes
		Nicholas Nye
		Nod
		The Listeners
		Bunches of Grapes
		The Truants
		Song of the Mad Prince
		Silver
		The House of Dreams
Jupiter JUR.00A1 An anthology	Christopher Hassall	*All That's Past*
	V. Clinton-Baddeley	*Railway Junction*
	Jill Balcon	*Silver*
	V. Clinton-Baddeley	*Song of the Mad Prince*
	Carleton Hobbs	*The Owl*
Jupiter JUR.00A4 An anthology	Marius Goring	*Old Shellover*
Jupiter JUR.00A9	C. Day Lewis	*All That's Past*
Jupiter JUR.00B1 An anthology	V. Clinton-Baddeley	*Five Eyes*
		Off the Ground
Caedmon T.C.1061	Dylan Thomas	*The Bards*
Jupiter JUR.00B2 An anthology	V. Clinton-Baddeley, Pauline Letts and Christopher Hassall	*The Ghosts*

Jupiter JUR.00B3 An anthology	V. Clinton-Baddeley	*Sam*
Caedmon T.C.1046	Walter de la Mare himself	*Isn't it A Lovely Day?* (Prose) *A Little About Witches* (Prose) *Peace* *The Veil* *The Railway Junction* *England* *In A Library* *The Scribe* *Here I Sit* *To a Candle* *Music* *All That's Past* *Farewell* *Away* *The Princess:* (A Story)
Argo RG192 An anthology	Robert Donat	*Before Dawn*
Argo RG437 An anthology	Robert Donat	*All That's Past*
Argo EAF108 An anthology	Peter Oke	*The Sleeper*
HMV CLP1841 An anthology	Margaret Rawlings	*Dreamsong*